956.054
McC

SPRING

The Illusion of Islamic Democracy

FEVER

Andrew C. McCarthy

ENCOUNTER DIGITAL

ELMHURST PUBLIC LIBRARY
125 S. Prospect Avenue
Elmhurst, IL 60126-3298

Spring Fever: The Illusion of Islamic Democracy was first published as an ebook as part of the new Encounter Digital imprint.

© 2013 by Andrew C. McCarthy

All rights reserved. No part of this publication may be reproduced, stored in a retrieval system, or transmitted, in any form or by any means, electronic, mechanical, photocopying, recording, or otherwise, without the prior written permission of Encounter Books, 900 Broadway, Suite 601, New York, New York, 10003.

First American edition published in 2013 by Encounter Books, an activity of Encounter for Culture and Education, Inc., a nonprofit, tax exempt corporation. Encounter Books website address: www.encounterbooks.com

Manufactured in the United States and printed on acid-free paper. The paper used in this publication meets the minimum requirements of ANSI/NISO Z39.48 1992 (R 1997) (*Permanence of Paper*).

FIRST AMERICAN EDITION

LIBRARY OF CONGRESS CATALOGING-IN-PUBLICATION DATA
McCarthy, Andrew C.
Spring fever/by Andrew C. McCarthy.
pages cm
ISBN 978-1-59403-691-0 (pbk: alk. paper)—ISBN 978-1-59403-644-6 (ebook)
1. Arab Spring, 2010- 2. Democracy—Arab countries. 3. Democracy—Religious aspects—Islam. 4. Islamic law—Political aspects. 5. Islam and state—Arab countries. 6. Islam and politics—Arab countries. 7. Islamic fundamentalism—Arab countries. 8. Arab countries—Foreign relations—United States. 9. United States—Foreign relations—Arab countries. I. Title.
JQ1850.A91M44 2012
321.80917'4927—dc23

2012041113

For Alexandra

CONTENTS

CONTENTS

TABLE OF ABBREVIATIONS

AKP	Justice and Development Party (Adalet ve Kalkinma Partisi) (Turkey)
CAIR	Council on American-Islamic Relations
EU	European Union
FCNA	Fiqh Council of North America
GSISS	Graduate School of Islamic and Social Sciences at Cordoba University in Virginia
IHH	Humanitarian Relief Foundation or IHH (İnsan Hak ve Hürriyetleri ve İnsani Yardım Vakfı)
IIIT	International Institute of Islamic Thought
ISNA	Islamic Society of North America
MSA	Muslim Students Association
NASA	National Aeronautics and Space Administration
NATO	North Atlantic Treaty Organization
NSP	National Salvation Party (Turkey)

TABLE OF ABBREVATIONS

OIC	Organization of Islamic Cooperation (formerly, Organization of the Islamic Conference)
PIJ	Palestinian Islamic Jihad
PLO	Palestine Liberation Organization
SCAF	Supreme Council of the Armed Forces (Egypt's post-Mubarak transitional government)
SCF	Sharia Compliant Finance
SPEC	Supreme Presidential Election Commission (Egypt)
USCIRF	United States Commission on International Religious Freedom
WAMY	World Assembly of Muslim Youth
WISE	World Islamic Study Enterprise

PREFACE

Well, that didn't take very long. On August 12, 2012, six weeks after being elected president of Egypt, Muslim Brotherhood leader Mohamed Morsi forced the resignations of the generals atop the ruling military junta. Effectively, his election has converted Egypt from a military dictatorship to a sharia dictatorship. As this book argues, that is the end to which "Islamic democracy" leads.

Although most of the manuscript of *Spring Fever: The Illusion of Islamic Democracy* was in the can by the late Spring of 2012, I delayed completing it until July. The Egyptian presidential election, such a big part of the "Arab Spring" story, was not decided until late June. The presidential election followed hard on both a national referendum on constitutional amendments and the parliamentary elections, all won by the Muslim Brotherhood and its fellow Islamic supremacists in lopsided fashion. "Islamic democracy" enthusiasts ascribe great significance to elections, taking them to mark real democratic progress, regardless of how bereft of real democratic culture the voting society is. It thus made sense to see through the historic electoral process before publishing this book.

Spring Fever, after all, is meant to be your antidote for the obsession that has become conventional American wisdom: the obdurate portrayal of the "Arab Spring" as a triumph of freedom. In reality, it is the ascendancy of Islamic supremacism. It follows a predictable path toward Islamization already trod in Turkey. The pattern is certain to proceed much more rapidly in the Muslim Middle East, which, unlike Turkey, has never sought to Westernize or to suppress Islam's supremacist tendencies.

In Egypt, the tension mounted this summer as the Supreme Council of the Armed Forces (SCAF), the military junta that seized control after Hosni Mubarak's fall from power, permitted the presidential election to go forward. By then, it was manifest that the Brotherhood's Morsi would win the presidency—absent a rigging of the election in favor of the junta's preferred candidate, Ahmed Shafiq, a vestige of the Mubarak regime.

Like Turkey's generals before them, SCAF did not have the stomach for a full-scale *coup d'état*. So the Egyptian generals tried their own version of Turkey's 1997 "Postmodern Coup": They stopped short of formally seizing total control, trying instead to assert *de facto* control without its looking too much like a military takeover, that bane of Western progressive piety. SCAF nullified the Islamic supremacists' parliamentary victory—with the fig leaf that the generals were merely enforcing a judicial ruling, not grabbing legislative authority for themselves. SCAF declared that the generals, not the newly elected legislature (i.e., not the Muslim Brotherhood), would oversee the drafting of a new constitution—although intermediaries would do the actual writing. And SCAF ensured that the military's continuing grip on political and economic power would render the new president substantially impotent—even though the president would be allowed to assume his largely ceremonial office and meet with world leaders as if he were a peer. Only with these precautions in place was the victory of the Brotherhood's presidential candidate announced.

Turkey's Islamist prime minister, Recep Tayyip Erdogan, is a principal focus of *Spring Fever*. Like Erdogan, Morsi assumed his office carefully. He took a deferential posture toward SCAF, realizing that the armed forces might crush him if he moved too quickly. Yet, again like Erdogan, he perceived his opposition's glass jaw, betrayed by the generals' palpable reluctance to crush him when they had the chance.

Morsi shrewdly took the ground the generals were willing to cede. He took office with great fanfare in the international media, swiftly began making governmental pronouncements, quietly courted allies in the ousted Parliament, and arranged one-on-one meetings with regional sovereigns and the American Secretary of State. These steps enhanced his global prestige, appearing to put him on a par with the people actually running the country.

Meanwhile, the new president announced policy goals that were certain to intensify his political support among Egyptians but unlikely to nettle SCAF. He called for a more rigorous application of classical sharia. He promised to pressure the United States to release the "Blind Sheikh"—Omar Abdel Rahman, the prominent Egyptian jihadist serving a sentence of life-imprisonment after his U.S. conviction on terrorism charges. And Morsi issued a pardon decree for 572 "political" prisoners serving prison sentences imposed by the Mubarak regime, including dozens of terrorist organization leaders—a gambit difficult for SCAF to oppose since, to appease the Islamist masses after the Tahrir Square uprising, the generals themselves had released many such prisoners, including Mohamed al-Zawahiri, brother of the al Qaeda leader Ayman al-Zawahiri.

As Morsi skillfully played this inside game, he counted on outside help from the Brotherhood-friendly Obama administration, just as Erdogan has in Turkey. Obama delivered. SCAF was badly undercut when Secretary of State Hillary Clinton publicly called for the generals to surrender power to Morsi. The new president also received a coveted invitation from President Obama to visit the White House in September. In its stubborn determination to spin the Brotherhood's disastrous rise as a victory for American democracy-promotion, the administration was not to be dissuaded—not by the Brotherhood's open hostility toward the United States; not by the stinging rebukes of Obama's performance by authentic Egyptian democrats, demoralized over America's infatuation with the Islamists. This, too, mirrored the Islamist ascendancy in Turkey: the more unabashed Erdogan became in promoting sharia and the Brotherhood's jihad against Israel, the closer Washington drew to him.

Meantime, Morsi's Brotherhood confederates assumed an increasingly hostile posture toward Israel. Brotherhood Supreme Guide Mohammed Badi, who had called for jihad against the United States in late 2010, publicly admonished Muslims to fulfill their scripturally based duty to wage violent jihad against Israel until "the filth of the Zionists" is cleansed and "Muslim rule throughout beloved Palestine" is "impos[ed]." Suddenly, "sharia enforcers" took to the streets of Egypt, harassing women to don the veil and hew to other repressive strictures of Islamic law—just as they do in Saudi Arabia, where sharia is the law of the land. Indeed, with Ramadan—the month Muslims consider sacred—falling in July this year, a sharia-based edict was announced, prohibiting Egyptians from eating during the daylight fasting hours. All the while, the persecution of Coptic Christians continuedapace. As happened in Turkey, culture, law, and international muscle patently trended toward Egypt's new Islamist leader and away from the armed forces.

There then occurred an event which dramatically undermined SCAF's political support, a development that readers of *Spring Fever* will find was inevitable. The only mild surprise here is the speed at which it happened.

On August 5, Gaza-based jihadists, using anti-tank rockets and gunfire, killed sixteen Egyptian soldiers in northern Sinai. The terrorists then commandeered two armored personnel carriers, attempting to attack Israel by driving them through the Karem Shalom crossing. They were stopped by Israeli Defense Forces. The IDF's aerial and ground attacks, which obliterated the would-be attackers, indicated that Israel had good enough intelligence to be prepared and to launch a decisive counterattack.

The incident profoundly embarrassed SCAF on a number of levels. The military is among the most revered institutions in Egyptian life. The public was thus horrified by its seeming ineptitude, particularly when it had taken such a central role in the nation's governance. Moreover, as the last year's electoral results have proven time and again, and as readers of *Spring Fever* will see, most Egyptians are beholden to the classical Islamic supremacism of the Middle East. Consequently, they regard Israel as the enemy. It offends them that their Muslim army, stationed on the Sinai border, is shooting it out with brave mujahideen fighting in Allah's cause—which is how they lionize jihadists who attack Israel. In the Egyptian mind, the armed forces should be helping destroy the Zionist entity, not helping shore up Israel's ramparts. And then there is the intelligence problem: To an Islamist, it can never be that Israel is extraordinarily effective in its self-defense; if the IDF was prepared to meet aggressors, and even to warn its citizens to take precautions, it can only be because the Mossad orchestrated the whole episode.

So it was that Egyptians fulminated over the killing of their troops and the quick work the IDF made of the jihadist "martyrs." The Muslim Brotherhood, echoed by the terrorist organization Hamas (the Brotherhood's Palestinian branch) and the Egyptian press, claimed that the attack "could be attributed to the Mossad, which has been seeking to abort the Egyptian revolution." Meanwhile, the "Shura Mujahideen Council," a previously unidentified group based in the Sinai border region—which has become a terrorist haven since Mubarak's ouster—claimed responsibility for the plot. The jihadists proclaimed: "There is no place in the Arab and Muslim world for liberal and secular democratic values," and that they were "dedicated to the struggle against Zionism."

The public anger at SCAF, seen as the enforcer of the unpopular Camp David peace treaty with Israel, handed Morsi an opportunity. Like Erdogan, he was quick to capitalize. Fearing a reprise of the Tahrir Square riots, the generals agreed to consult with Morsi, whom they previously sought to marginalize. The consultation proved fateful: Field Marshal Mohamed Hussein Tantawi—Mubarak's right hand as defense minister and, effectively, the leader of SCAF—abruptly announced his retirement. So did several other prominent military officials. Taking a page out of the Erdogan playbook, Morsi maneuvered himself into the upper-hand position of naming their replacements.

Of at least equal significance, Morsi unilaterally declared null and void the decree by which SCAF purported to gut presidential authority. In its place, he issued an edict vesting himself with broad legislative and executive authority, as well as effective control over the drafting of a new constitution. This was not a restoration of the "democratic" status quo: a presidential spokesman was quick to explain that Morsi had no intention of reinstating the recently elected Parliament, nor would he honor the result of last year's popular referendum, which deferred the writing of the constitution until after the newly elected president *and legislature* were in place.

No, Morsi, the Brotherhood's point-man, would take care of the constitution on his own, thank you very much. Of course, to control the promulgation of Egypt's fundamental law—to ensure that, as Morsi promised during the campaign, it would reflect "the sharia, then the sharia, and finally, the sharia"—has been the Brotherhood's highest priority since the first elections. Indeed, it has been the Brotherhood's highest priority since Hassan al-Banna founded the organization almost ninety years ago.

As "Islamic democracy" inexorably installs sharia totalitarianism in Egypt, Erdogan proceeds, under the same "democracy" banner, to re-Islamize Turkey. Thus, sharia's repression of Turkish women worsens. The regime recently conceded that "gender-based violence" is now the leading cause of death in the country for women aged 15 to 44—surpassing cancer, traffic accidents, war, and malaria. In Syria to the south, Erdogan—complemented by aid from the Obama administration, the Saudis, and Qatar, as well as al Qaedamuscle—has maneuvered the Brotherhood into command of the opposition now warring against the teetering dictator, Bashar al-Assad. Just as in Egypt, the rise of Islamic supremacists in the Syrian opposition has meant an escalation in the persecution of Christians. Moreover, sharia is expanding its grip in the new "Islamic democracies" of Libyaand Tunisia. And to the east, the Obama administration is pleading with the Taliban to come to the negotiating table with an eye toward participating in the government of Afghanistan.

Recall that it was to prevent the return of the Taliban—its cruel enforcement of sharia and its alliance with al Qaeda—that the United States has remained in Afghanistan, at an enormous sacrifice of blood and treasure, for over a decade since routing al Qaeda's forces there in the weeks after 9/11. Now, with "Islamic democracy" in the air, not only is the Taliban's return more likely by the day; Hamid Karzai, the U.S.-backed Afghan president, has even suggested that Mullah Omar, the Taliban leader, run for president in the next election. This, too, makes perfect sense. The Taliban could comfortably restore their repressive sharia regime without having to change a comma of the new constitution the U.S. State Department helped post-Taliban (and perhaps pre-Taliban) Afghanistan write: a "democratic" constitution that establishes Islam as the state religion and installs sharia as fundamental law.

Spring Fever: it's infectious.

CHAPTER ONE

The Train

"Democracy is just the train we board to reach our destination." So said Recep Tayyip Erdogan in 1998, four years before the train arrived at his station—which is to say, four years before his Islamic supremacist party rode the democratic electoral process to dominance over Turkey. It was the train that enabled Erdogan, only recently jailed as a seditionist, to be installed as prime minister. It was the train that enabled him to begin hollowing out the culture of true democracy, supplanting it with the chimera known as "Islamic democracy."

Alas, Turkey's rising strongman understands the democracy fetish far better than our democracy crusaders do. For him, "Islamic democracy" has proved to be an extraordinarily useful fairy tale. And the prime minister knows that one civilization's useful fairy tale is another civilization's nightmare.

To the south and east of Ankara, with detours through progressive Western capitals and their puppy dog media, the fairy tale currently masquerades as the "Arab Spring." It is a luscious rainbow garden of "Revolution": Cedar in Lebanon, Jasmine in Tunisia,

Lotus in Egypt, streaming Purples and bursting Blues in Iraq and Kuwait. But the first and still the most prominent "Arab Spring" was not Arab at all, though it was, of course, Islamic. *That's* what those in the grip of Spring Fever are getting at: the dream that *Islam* and authentic democracy, *Western* democracy, are seamlessly compatible. The "Arab" part is almost beside the point. Thus, the paragon of "Islamic democracy" is the "Turkish model," pioneered by Erdogan and his collaborators, the Muslim Brotherhood.

Right off the bat, we learn two things. First, the chimera must always be camouflaged in high-flown rhetoric and bright, euphoric hues, but retain the patina of muscular secularism that Turkey—*pre-Erdogan Turkey*—evoked for nearly a century. Otherwise, the illusion might be seen for what it truly is: the unshackling of Islamic suprem-acism, the very enemy of democracy, that Kemal Ataturk labored to place under wraps. Second, the wrenching thing about this illusion is that, even before it evaporates in the crucible of harsh reality, we know how the fairy tale must end. Oh, there will be surprising twists and turns along the way, as there are in any human enterprise. But the trend-lines are unmistakable, the trajectory of change more cer-tain than its pace. The outcome is not in doubt because the outcome has already happened.

That was in Turkey.

Erdogan, the train conductor, is not just a master of metaphor. He is a trailblazer: a Muslim Brother who drank deep the lessons of the master, Hassan al-Banna—the charismatic Egyptian schoolteacher who founded the Muslim Brotherhood. Banna's Islamic suprema-cism came in direct response to Ataturk, his hated contemporary. It was Ataturk who purged Islam from the public square, secularized Turkish society, and dragged a plenary Muslim population kicking and screaming into the embrace of the West. It is Ataturk whose Turkey Erdogan is determined to "fundamentally transform"—if we may borrow that fitting phrase from the Turkish prime minister's close friend and power-politics soul-mate, Barack Obama.

CULTURE IS EVERYTHING

Erdogan's transformation of Turkey has been achieved, just as the
Brotherhood's broader goal of regional hegemony is now attainable,
because he, like the Brothers, fully grasps Banna's core teaching: Culture is everything. Regardless of what laws may say and dictators may
decree, Islamic supremacism—after three generations of disciplined,
lushly financed, bottom-up cultivation—is the dynamic culture of
the Middle East. Besides explaining the defeat of Kemalism, Islamic
culture—reflecting a *civilization* fundamentally different from the
West, one that refutes the universalist pretensions of progressives—is
the driving force behind today's Islamist ascendancy.

The modern West obsesses over politics and law. We are mes-
merized, in particular, by their procedural aspects: popular elections,
constitution-writing, and the like. We seem to have forgotten that
the American people, to take the example closest to home, was a
distinct cultural phenomenon for well over a century before shots
rang out at Lexington and Concord. Our signature commitment to
individual liberty, free markets, and limited government shaped our
law and our politics—not the other way around. Politics and law
can dominate culture only with an iron fist, and only for a time, if
that iron fist fails to change the culture. Ataturk, in the end, merely
suppressed culture; he failed to change it. It was stronger than the
rickety secular castle he undertook to construct over its deep civilizational roots.

The Muslim Brotherhood represents the culture that Ataturk
could not tame. The Brothers see themselves as the vanguard of a
civilizational mass movement, shepherds of what and how a society
thinks. That vision pervades Islam's centers of global influence: the
Organization of Islamic Cooperation, an alliance of fifty-seven Muslim
sovereigns—counting the Palestinian authority, which Muslims regard
as a "state"; and storied al-Azhar University, the center of Sunni jurisprudence since the tenth century. The result is that Muslims in the

current of this Islamic mainstream perceive themselves as members of a global community, the ummah, rather than anything so pedestrian as a nationalist entity, or even a neo-Ottoman or pan-Arabic entity.

It takes a long time to dominate a culture, even if the project is more in the nature of revitalizing a centuries-old cultural core, as opposed to Ataturk's attempt to impose something new and alien. To dominate culture takes a patient, relentless plan that resonates with the popular spirit.

Banna's was such a plan. It called for a ground-up march through society's institutions. First, the Muslim individual would be steeped in the principles of Salafism—a fundamentalist brand of Sunni Islam modeled on the founding generations. With this inculcation in place, the Brotherhood would build outward: from the indoctrinated individual to indoctrinated families, communities, enclaves, towns, cities, and so on.

To lay such a foundation is the work of generations. Once laid, though, the program's tentacles grip society—animating the young and energetic, while the lethargic masses become gradually resigned to it. To carry the project off does not take a majority or anything close to it; just a purposeful faction disciplined enough to intimidate and infiltrate society's influential institutions. To control the culture in this way is to dictate the course of politics and law, to put the procedures of politics and law in the service of culture. If democracy is in vogue, as it is today—in name, if not in substance—its procedures become the train that chugs the society toward Islamization, toward the goal of re-establishing the caliphate.

That is what is happening now. That is why, many decades after their deaths, Banna has his victory over Ataturk.

To understand the "Arab Spring," it is essential first and foremost to grasp that the key fact on the ground in Arab countries—as well as in Turkey, Iran, Pakistan, Afghanistan, and other neighboring non-Arab territories—is Islam. It is not poverty, illiteracy, or the lack of modern democratic institutions. These features, like anti-Semitism, anti-Americanism, and an insular propensity to buy into conspiracy theories featuring infidel villains, are epiphenomena. They are *consequences* of Islam's regional dominance and supremacist ambitions. They do not *cause* populations to turn to Islam. One does not need to be led to that which pervades one's existence.

What kind of Islam are we talking about? Well, that may be a complex question in circumstances where Islam attempts to move beyond the horizons of its geographical dominance—although even in the West, where Muslims remain a small minority, the question becomes less complex as Muslims amass numbers and strength. As that happens, their leaders inexorably turn more confrontational and doctrinaire; their rank-and-file feel ever greater pressure to follow suit, or at least muffle their misgivings.

With the "Arab Spring," though, we are not talking about an Islam under pressure to evolve, to make the compromises that integration in a different civilization calls for. We are talking about Islam on its home turf.

In the Muslim Middle East, the dispositive Islam is supremacist Islam. That is not to say there aren't different Islamic sects. The important ones, though, divide mainly on the method by which Islam should come to dominate, not on whether it should dominate. On the latter, they have no doubt.

On its native soil, Islam is most emphatically not "moderate," notwithstanding its Western apologists' risible insistence that moderation is Islam's defining characteristic. In fact, in a 2007 interview that has gotten next to no attention, Prime Minister Erdogan recoiled at the very term "moderate Islam." "These descriptions are very ugly," he seethed, "it is offensive and an insult to our religion. There is no moderate or immoderate Islam. Islam is Islam, and that's it."

This Islam is at once insular and ambitiously aggressive. Recall Erdogan's allusion to democracy as the "train" to Islamization. It is worth quoting, and bearing in mind throughout the chapters that follow, the very next thing said by the man who is now Islam's most significant presence in world politics—the man Western chancelleries insist on portraying as a "moderate" ally even as he venomously reproves the very idea and exhorts Muslims in the West to resist assimilation: "The mosques are our barracks, the minarets our bayonets, the cupolas our helmets and the faithful our soldiers."

Moderation indeed.

IT'S A "RELIGION," SO IT MUST BE GOOD

In the West, democracy is not just elections and constitution-writing. When we invoke "democracy"—at least those of us who venerate it, as opposed to seeing it as a ring of gold fit for a swine's snout—we mean it as a shorthand description of a culture based on freedom. Our democracy connotes the equal dignity of each individual, self-determination, and reason. To the Muslim architects of the "Arab Spring," by contrast, "democracy" is a mere vehicle, a procedural path of least resistance to a radically different way of life. Islamic civilization is not merely an exotic splash on the gorgeous global mosaic with a few embarrassingly archaic eccentricities. It is an entirely different way of looking at the world.

In the West, we struggle with this disconcerting truth. It defies our end-of-history smugness. Enraptured by diversity for its own sake, we have lost the capacity to comprehend a civilization whose idea of "diversity" is to coerce diverse peoples into obeying its evolution-resistant norms, particularly its non-negotiable prohibition against free expression that takes the form of critical examination of Islam. The free-wheeling discourse, the sometimes heated, hostile, provocative, and even obnoxious exchange of ideas that is so mundane, yet vital, in a culture of liberty is, in the Muslim worldview, the outrage of "defamation" . . . and, when it comes to exchanging ideas about Islam, truth is no defense.

The modern West is unwilling to process the possibility, much less the inevitability, that what is diverse might, in fact, be unwelcome. Unwilling to be judgmental about anything—except that any concern about Islamic supremacism must be "Islamophobic"—our intelligentsia sets about remaking Islam in its own progressive self-image: The noble, ur-tolerant Religion of Peace. No point wrapping our brains around the possibility that there just might be doctrinal differences between sects and belief systems that render them unsuited to clement coexistence. That would contradict our one-size-fits-all assumptions about "the world's great religions"—the label thoughtlessly affixed by elites who, outside their trendy Islamophilia, get pretty damn phobic when fretting over evangelicals, the Catholic Church, "the religious right," and all those cagey Jews.

In the modern West, discussions of "religion" are as vapid as invocations of "democracy." As the mindless banter goes, "It's all good." All "religion" is peaceful and loving and uplifting and tolerant. And Islam is a religion, so that's what Islam must be, right? The countless strands of the ummah that refuse to go along with the program are miniaturized. They are assigned labels that scream *fringe!*: Islamist, fundamentalist, Salafist, Wahhabist, radical, jihadist, extremist, militant, or, of course, "conservative" Muslims who adhere to "political Islam." Allah forbid we should notice that, when you stack all these "fringes" end-to-end, there isn't much daylight for the blooming of moderation.

We pretend that Muslims who accurately invoke Islamic scripture in the course of forcibly imposing the dictates of classical sharia—the Islamic legal and political system—are engaged in "anti-Islamic activity," as Britain's former home secretary Jacqui Smith memorably put it. When the ongoing Islamization campaign is advanced by violence, as inevitably happens, we risibly maintain that this aggression cannot have been ideologically driven. Surely some American policy or Israeli act of self-defense is to blame.

But could these possibly be rationales for the murderous jihad waged by Boko Haram Muslims against Nigerian Christians or by Egyptian Muslims against Egyptian Copts? Are Indonesian and Pakistani Muslims really persecuting Ahmadi Muslims because they're mad about Israel's American-backed "apartheid" against the Palestinians? Does that have anything to do with the internecine warring between Sunnis and Shiites—a ferocious tradition nearly as old as Islam itself, and one that, as night follows day, has been renewed in Iraq upon the recent departure of American troops?

No, of course not. The aggression is explicable only if we acknowledge the totalitarian thrust that animates mainstream Islam in the Middle East. We need not discount the existence of real Muslim democrats or abandon the hope for Islamic reform. There *are* Muslim democrats, and there *is* hope for Islamic reform. To be sure, the democrats are vastly outnumbered and the potential for reform, at least in the short term, is paltry. But they and it are real. That, however, is beside the point. For our own sake, America and the West need to start seeing this part of the world as it is, not as we would have it.

The main lesson of the Arab Spring is that the mirage of Islam as a moderating force hospitable to democratic transformation exists solely in our own minds, for our own consumption. The Muslims of the Middle East take no note of our reimagining their belief system. In the main, if not affirmatively hostile toward Western overtures, these Muslims are oblivious. They do not care what we think. They do not measure themselves against Western standards and perceptions. They study what the West thinks, they exploit what the West holds dear, but in no wise are they inhibited by Western norms.

"The underlying problem for the West is not Islamic fundamentalism," wrote Samuel Huntington. "It is Islam, a different civilization whose people are convinced of the superiority of their culture." Not convinced merely in the passive sense of assuming that they will triumph in the end; Muslim leaders are galvanized by what they take to be a divinely ordained mission of proselytism. The indoctrination they have in mind is not limited to spiritual principles; it encompasses an all-purpose societal code prescribing rules for everything from warfare and finance to social interaction and personal hygiene.

The historian Andrew Bostom notes that in the World War I era, even as the Ottoman Empire collapsed and Ataturk symbolically extinguished the caliphate, C. Snouck Hurgronje, then the West's leading scholar of Islam, marveled that Muslims remained broadly confident in what he called the "idea of universal conquest." In Islam's darkest hour, this conviction remained "a central point of union against the unfaithful."

It looms more powerful in today's Islamic ascendancy. But we'll miss it if we don't shake the epidemic of Spring Fever.

CHAPTER TWO

Totalitarian Democracy

The "Islamic democracy" that the United States has birthed in Baghdad ranks among the world's worst offenders when it comes to the persecution of religious minorities. According to the United States Commission on International Religious Freedom's Fourteenth Annual Report, released on March 20, 2012, Iraq is among the sixteen countries assessed as the most egregious and systematic religious freedom violators.

Homosexuals fare no better. This, no doubt, owes to the teaching of Ayatollah Ali Sistani, Iraq's most authoritative voice on sharia and, perhaps, Shia Islam's most influential jurist. Sistani proclaims that "sodomy and lesbianism" are not merely "forbidden"; "sodomites," he adds, "should be killed in the worst manner possible." Again, this is not al Qaeda or Hezbollah talking; this is Iraq's leading cleric, who is regarded by the United States government as a key supporter of its Islamic democracy project. It is a project Sistani supported not because he believes in *democracy* but because he believes in *sharia*. Iraq's Shiites had the numbers to make a sharia state happen in a popular election. Sistani, by the way, also instructs Muslims to avoid physical contact with non-Muslims, whom he analogizes to "urine, feces, semen, dead bodies, blood, dogs, pigs, alcoholic liquors," and "the sweat of an animal who persistently eats filth." Hard to imagine how a country profoundly influenced by such a man could possibly find itself cited by the Commission for persecuting minorities, no?

The Islamic democracy in Pakistan also made the Commission's list of persecutors. Islamabad was cited for its "engage[ment] in and tolerat[ion] of ongoing, and egregious violations of freedom of religion or belief." This was due, in particular, to its rampant anti-Semitism, complemented by its "repressive blasphemy laws and other religiously discriminatory legislation." The latter pointedly targets the Ahmadi, a minority Muslim sect whose members, the Commission observed, are "increasingly subject to abuse and . . . sentenced to death and even executed for the capital crime of—waging war against God." The Ahmadi, it is worth noting, are also persecuted in Indonesia, the world's largest Islamic country by population and most moderate Islamic country by reputation.

Back before March Madness gave way to Spring Fever, if you filled out your brackets and had the new Islamic democracy in Egypt making the Commission's Not So Sweet Sixteen, you were prescient. "Over the last year"—i.e., amid the delusional Western media coverage of the vibrant, hopeful "Arab Spring"—the Commission found that "[v]iolence targeting Coptic Orthodox Christians increased significantly," contributing to the country's overall "systematic, ongoing, and egregious violations of freedom of thought, conscience and religion or belief."

The Commission noted that the military junta governing Egypt since the ouster of Hosni Mubarak had "failed to protect religious minorities from violent attacks at a time when minority communities have been increasingly vulnerable." Yet, the commissioners omitted to further elucidate the obvious: The forces responsible for these violent attacks and the climate that fosters them—the Muslim

Brotherhood and the so-called "Salafists"—are the very factions that Egyptians, in their "democratic process," overwhelmingly chose to run the country.

Moreover, despite being rabidly anti-Western, these factions perversely enjoy the support of Western governments. So enthralled are Western leaders by the illusion of Islamic democracy that they ignore what its reality means for the minorities certain to be abused and put to flight. The United States and Europe now pressure Egypt's transitional military junta to hurry along and transfer power to the duly elected Sunni supremacists.

The Turks, our great friends and, yes, NATO partners, are also in the Commission's Hall of Shame. Besides rounding up, imprisoning, and prosecuting dissenting military officers, politicians and journalists, the Commission found that Erdogan's government—now entering its second decade of control—systematically and egregiously slashes the religious liberty of non-Muslims.

The bottom rung countries also include the two in which sharia is fully established as the law of the land. The first is the heinously repressive Saudi regime, which the United States government sees as its "moderate" ally despite the Saudis' decades' long global campaign to propagate their virulently anti-Western construction of Islam. The second is the heinously repressive Iranian regime, which the United States sees just as Iran sees itself: America's mortal enemy. Iran, too, pretends to be a democracy. The Saudis, for all their affectations of enlightenment do not go that far—sure, some women are now permitted to work (selling women's apparel) and even run for public office, but they still face the sharia penalty of scourging if they try to drive themselves to these jobs.

Meanwhile, in Afghanistan, where tens of thousands of American troops still risk their lives to prop up the regime of President Hamid Karzai, at least two men have been put on capital trial for apostatizing from Islam. Under the classical interpretation of sharia, relying on not only Koranic verses but also an admonitory hadith quoting Mohammed himself (Bukhari, vol. 9, no. 57: "Whoever changes his Islamic religion, kill him"), a Muslim who renounces Islam must receive the death penalty.

The Muslim Brotherhood's top jurist, Yusuf al-Qaradawi, probably the most influential Sunni cleric in the world, posits that apostates are "the gravest danger" to Islamic society; therefore, Muslims must snuff them out lest their ideas "spread like wildfire on a field of thorns." And on this matter, Sheikh Qaradawi is what passes for a "moderate": he distinguishes *private* apostasy—though he finds it condemnable, he thinks mere ostracism is a sufficient penalty. (It is not exactly clear how the apostasy stays "private" if the community knows enough about it to ostracize the apostate—details, details.) For public apostasy, though, Qaradawi stands with the overwhelming weight of Islamic authority: "The punishment . . . is execution."

Indeed, *Reliance of the Traveller—A Classic Manual of Islamic Law*, endorsed by both al-Azhar University sharia scholars and the Muslim Brotherhood's top think-tank, the International Institute of Islamic Thought, instructs that apostasy is not merely "the ugliest form of disbelief," but one of only three offenses that justify the killing of a Muslim.[1] As it did in Iraq, the U.S. State Department helped draft the new constitution of Afghanistan, which establishes Islam as the state religion and installs sharia as a primary source of law.

NO SECULARISM IN ISLAM
Why does this happen? Why do Islamic countries systematically abuse non-Muslims and even minority Muslim sects? Why, in fact,

---

1. The others are adultery and murder of a Muslim. See Ahmad ibn Naquib al-Masri, *Reliance of the Traveller—A Classic Manual of Islamic Sacred Law* (*'Umdat al-Salik*) (Translation published by Amana Publications, 1991), Sec. o1.0 "Who Is Subject to Retaliation For Injurious Crimes," and Sec. o8.0 "Apostasy From Islam (Ridda)"; see also, e.g., "Answering Islam.org, "The Punishment for Apostasy from Islam" (Jan. 4, 2007) (Silas).

do countries like Iraq and Egypt become even more repressive of religious liberty as they become more "democratic"?

Most of the explanation is straightforward. In the pre-"democratic" dictatorships that dominated "Arab Spring" countries, the main targets of repression were political enemies of the regime. Saddam Hussein and Hosni Mubarak, to take two prime examples, were interested in enriching themselves while having their commands obeyed. True, Islamic culture was a fact of life in their realms, and therefore occasional accommodation of Islamic activists and lip-service to Islamic traditions were in their interests. They were not, however, propagating a belief system—the dictator believes only in his own power.

Islamic supremacism is crucially different. Not only does it yearn for domination; it is substantively hostile to non-adherents. It regards as threatening anything that is not Islam, and thus it regards as anathema the very notion of "secular space" in a civil society, separate from Islam's precepts. Indeed, let's say it emphatically: "Secularism can never enjoy a general acceptance in an Islamic society."

Now, someone is going to read that last sentence and say, "Bingo! There's your proof. McCarthy is a hopelessly bigoted, raging Islamophobe!" Now, I could just bat my eyes and say, "Gee, I get that all the time." But on this occasion, I'll simply point out that, while I have no doubt it is true that "secularism can never enjoy general acceptance in an Islamic society," those words are not mine. I was quoting none other than Sheikh Qaradawi.

He made this straightforward assertion in his book, *How the Imported Solutions Disastrously Affected Our Ummah*, an excerpt of which was published by the *Saudi Gazette* back in 2010. The renowned scholar's rationale is worth excerpting:

As Islam is a comprehensive system of worship (Ibadah) and legislation (Shari'ah), the acceptance of secularism means abandonment of Shari'ah, a denial of the divine guidance and a rejection of Allah's injunctions. It is indeed a false claim that Shari'ah is not proper to the requirements of the present age. The acceptance of a legislation formulated by humans means a preference of the humans' limited knowledge and experiences to the divine guidance: "Say! Do you know better than Allah?" (Qur'an, 2:140) For this reason, *the call for secularism among Muslims is atheism and a rejection of Islam. Its acceptance as a basis for rule in place of Shari'ah is downright apostasy.* [Emphasis added.]

We probably do not need reminding that apostasy is an offense sharia punishes by death. Is it any wonder that the more Islamic supremacist ideology controls a society, the more certain it is that non-Muslims and Muslim minorities will be oppressed?

Islamic supremacism is just a different kind of dictatorship. By comparison to secular dictatorship, it is actually *more* totalitarian because Islamic supremacism is about not the personal aggrandizement of the rulers. It is about the imposition of a comprehensive social system that governs life down to the most granular details.

So how could a region's increasing envelopment by Islamic supremacism and its sharia code be seen as a "democratic" transformation by progressives? Before answering, it is worth pausing to clarify two things.

First, on sharia, we are again talking about Islam on its home turf, where the classical, fundamentalist construction of sharia, as straightforwardly outlined in *Reliance of the Traveller*, is dominant. I do not contend that sharia is monolithic. There are less severe interpretations. There are more nuanced explications that, as lawyers are wont to do, fixate more on centuries of sharia jurisprudence than on the literal scriptures that this jurisprudence construes—the hope being that modernist jurists can, by their rulings, lend an elasticity that the hidebound doctrine itself lacks, and thus evolve it. There are, in addition, courageous Muslim reformers, particularly in the West, who seek to inject in sharia the West's Judeo-Christian "Render unto

16

Caesar" tradition of separating the spiritual realm from the state's compulsive authority.

Personally, I am not very optimistic about this modernization effort: dividing mosque and state seems to me like denying sharia the foundational principle that makes it sharia. But on this, as on many other things, I could be wrong . . . and I hope I am. Nevertheless, our hopefulness for reform, or for a jurisprudentially driven softening of sharia into something like a body of spiritual guidelines that does not prescribe controlling civil law, is mainly pertinent to Islam *in the West*. It has little contemporary relevance to the *Muslim Middle East*. There sharia means classical sharia, and the general population is at least decades away from meaningful penetration by rationalist academics and reformers.

Second, regarding *progressives*: By using the word, I do not mean to make a partisan attack against Democrats or the Obama administration. The progressive interventionism that dictates modern American foreign policy is a bipartisan phenomenon. Domestic policy is really no different: The Beltway's bipartisan political establishment—what Angelo Codevilla fittingly calls "the ruling class"—favors an expansive and evermore intrusive welfare state. Furthermore, while most modern progressives are unabashed people of the Left, they defy easy identification by party labels.

Adherents of the philosophy my friend John Fonte aptly coined as "Transnational Progressivism" are, with varying degrees of ardor, of a post-sovereign bent of mind. They favor multi-lateralist governance over national self-determinism based on a culture of individual liberty. This way of thinking is only slightly more predominant among Democrats than it is within the Republican establishment, although the more conservative and libertarian Republican base eschews it. Certainly since the late 1980s, the Tranzies, as the great John O'Sullivan deliciously refers to them, have reigned over the State Department, regardless of which party has held the White House. Our diplomats are at home in the Council on Foreign Relations,

Princeton's Woodrow Wilson Center, or Harvard's Kennedy School; for most of them, the thought of a speech on American exceptionalism, delivered by a Tea Party darling at, say, the Reagan Library, would induce febrile seizures.

THE "DEMOCRACY" MIRAGE

So why do transnational progressives, irrespective of their partisan affiliation, look at what is plainly an ascendancy of Islamic supremacism, a totalitarian program, and see instead what they call "Islamic democracy"?

Part of the answer, naturally, is political: the people in power in the West during the Middle East uprisings stand to be blamed for "losing Iraq," "losing Turkey," "losing Egypt," and the like. For their own sake, they need to spin failure as success, so better to frame a catastrophe as a "democracy"—it did, after all, feature popular elections and constitution-writing.

This is unfortunate. Contrary to popular belief, most of the things that happen in the world are not America's doing, nor is it within our capacity to dictate the outcome. The fact that we can often make things worse—as several American administrations have made the rise of Islamic supremacism worse—does not necessarily mean we could have prevented those things from happening. The "Arab Spring" is just such a phenomenon. It was going to happen, regardless of what we did or omitted to do. It has been coming for generations. The Muslim Brotherhood has not been idling for the last eighty-plus years; it has been putting into action Hassan al-Banna's blueprint for ground-up revolution. I'm not sure we ever could have stopped it, but, assuming we could have, that would have required taking decisive steps a long time ago. It is too late for that now.

Once Sunni supremacism rolled over Turkey's vigorous attempt to remake itself into a secular, pro-Western state, it was only a matter of time until the tide swept through the predominantly Arab Middle

East. America and Europe did not cause the Islamist ascendancy. Yes, Western leaders enabled and exacerbated it, but it is a homemade Islamic triumph, not a Western failure. It's a shame that Western politicians perceive the need to paint it as something it's not.

Then there are the eternal optimists who try to pass themselves off as hard-headed pragmatists. Their theory is that governing will make the ruler accountable to the public; consequently, the practical responsibilities of the offices to which they've been elected will tame Islamist politicians. They will evolve, coming to see that sharia and anti-Semitic, anti-Western animus are just not compatible with running a government in the modern world. Governing will transform them into moderates. (And here we thought they already were moderates!)

Sounds wonderful . . . except it's a theory in search of empirical confirmation. In fact, its proponents expect you to glide by its considerable empirical refutation. Has Iran gotten more moderate over the last thirty years? Has Hamas's election in Gaza—where they somehow haven't had an election since—helped that terrorist organization evolve? Has Hezbollah's achievement of electoral success in Lebanon changed Hezbollah, or has it instead given Iran's forward terrorist militia the cover of "democratic" legitimacy for its jihadist provocations? The election of Islamic supremacists in Turkey has moved that country toward extremism, not away from it. The election of Islamic supremacists in Iraq—who would not relinquish power even after they lost an election—has shifted that country into close alliance with Iran.

The theory does not work because it foolishly applies Western assumptions to the Islamic context. In the United States, we have a culture of individual liberty: The people are sovereign. As the inimitable Mark Steyn frequently points out, the officials we elect are our representatives, not our rulers. They are moved by the imperatives of governance to moderate or abandon extreme or implausible positions because they will be cashiered if they do not. President

Obama wanted to close the detention camp for jihadist enemy combatants at Guantanamo Bay and give 9/11 mastermind Khalid Sheikh Mohammed a civilian trial rather than a military commission. He did not follow through—not because he wants any less to do these things, but because he had to yield to popular disapproval if he wanted to remain politically viable. If his policies are sufficiently unpopular, he will be voted out of office and he will leave.

RULERS NOT REPRESENTATIVES

Islamic culture does not work that way. The new regimes may be popularly elected, but make no mistake: They will be rulers, not representatives. The installation of sharia is not window dressing. It is of significant political and cultural moment. In a sharia society, the leader is a ruler and his principal responsibility is fidelity to Allah's law, not to the parochial needs of his constituents. In fact, the principal responsibility of his constituents is also fidelity to Allah's law; their own needs and desires are secondary because the culture is premised not on individual liberty but on the solidarity of the ummah, to which the individual is expected to subordinate himself.

Writing in 1958, Princeton's eminent scholar of Islam Bernard Lewis highlighted this cultural gulf in explaining Islam's innate resistance to real democracy (an explanation which, as Andrew Bostom acidly observes, contradicts Professor Lewis's giddier takes on the prospects of Islamic democracy in later years):

> I turn now . . . to those [factors] deriving from the very nature
> of Islamic society, tradition, and thought. The first of these is the
> authoritarianism, perhaps we may even say the totalitarianism,
> of the Islamic political tradition. . . . Many attempts have been
> made to show that Islam and democracy are identical—attempts
> usually based on a misunderstanding of Islam or democracy or
> both. This sort of argument expresses a need of the up-rooted
> Muslim intellectual who is no longer satisfied with or capable of

understanding traditional Islamic values, and who tries to justify, or rather, re-state, his inherited faith in terms of the fashionable ideology of the day. It is an example of the romantic and apologetic presentation of Islam that is a recognized phase in the reaction of Muslim thought to the impact of the West. . . .

In point of fact, except for the early caliphate, when the anarchic individualism of tribal Arabia was still effective, the political history of Islam is one of almost unrelieved autocracy. . . . [I]t was authoritarian, often arbitrary, sometimes tyrannical. There are no parliaments or representative assemblies of any kind, no councils or communes, no chambers of nobility or estates, no municipalities in the history of Islam; nothing but the sovereign power, to which the subject owed complete and unwavering obedience as a religious duty imposed by the Holy Law.

This in fact goes a long way toward explaining why Islamic populations for so long tolerated dictatorships and why, when they are now sweeping dictatorships aside, it is only for an alternative that promises more authoritarianism—more adherence to sharia, not government more responsive to the private desires of individual citizens. As Lewis further recounted:

In the great days of classical Islam this duty [to obey] was only owed to the lawfully appointed caliph, as God's vicegerent on earth and head of the theocratic community, and then only for as long as he upheld the law; but with the decline of the caliphate and the growth of military dictatorship, Muslim jurists and theologians accommodated their teachings to the changed situation and extended the religious duty of obedience to any effective authority, however impious, however barbarous. For the last thousand years, the political thinking of Islam has been dominated by such maxims as "tyranny is better than anarchy" and "whose power is established, obedience to him is incumbent."

From a different angle, Professor Lewis was getting at the same reality reflected by Sheikh Qaradawi when the Muslim Brotherhood eminence was asked to explain his rationale for holding that sharia would not bar women from serving in parliament (as long as it was only a smattering of women such that they wouldn't actually be *running* parliament). "Legislation belongs to God," he explained, "and we only fill in the blanks."[2] There simply is not an understanding in sharia societies that *elected* government will be *representative* government. The elected official seamlessly becomes a strongman because he is not beholden to the will and aspirations of free, self-determining people. His triumph entitles him to wield the power of the state—including military force, if the military submits.

DEMOCRACY . . . BUT NOT FREEDOM

Finally, on the matter of democracy, there is a huge difference between the traditional, constitutional American concept and the progressive vision. Freedom is of minimal interest to progressives, certainly not *freedom* as is commonly understood: namely, the bedrock conceit that we are our own governors, autonomous over our own lives. To be clear, we are talking about freedom in a democracy, not an anarchy. In a rational social compact, freedom requires that we surrender a quantum of our independence to secure the nation and to honor the rudimentary norms of respect for life and property. If a free society is to flourish, nothing less than ordered liberty will do.

Alas, the "liberty" part of ordered liberty is more a nuisance than a value for progressives. The traditional rights to be free from government demands and to have government restricted to its expressly enumerated powers are a hindrance to their social engineering schemes. For the modern Left, in particular, the individual's freedom is a relic of a bygone time, when life was simpler and dominated by

---

2.   McCarthy, *The Grand Jihad*, p. 88.

sexist, slave-holding white men of a colonialist bent. In contrast to the Right's emphasis on *liberty*, focusing on what the state cannot do *to you*, the Left's métier is *rights*, what the state must do *for you*. Translation: what the state must *compel you to give to me*—with government handling both the confiscation and redistribution ends of the arrangement.

The late, vastly under-appreciated political scientist Jacob Lieb Talmon coined the phrase "totalitarian democracy" to describe the form of "political Messianism" that infected free societies in the twentieth century.[3] It was based, he asserted, on "the assumption of a sole and exclusive truth in politics." To the contrary, liberal democracy (in the classic sense of "liberal," which is antithetical to progressive notions of democracy) "assumes politics to be a matter of trial and error." It takes human beings as basically good but incorrigibly fallible; it sees their political systems as just another pragmatic contrivance in lives that for the most part are lived "altogether outside the sphere of politics."

The avatars of totalitarian democracy, by contrast, maintain that they have arrived at a sole and exclusive truth. For the liberal democrat, the essence of freedom is what Talmon described as "spontaneity and the absence of coercion. For the progressive, however, freedom is "realized only in the pursuit and attainment of an absolute collective purpose," rooted in the "sole and exclusive truth" they passionately believe they have discovered.

This "truth" comes to pervade human existence. The personal becomes the political because everything from the car you drive, to the clothes you wear, to the movies you watch becomes, as President Obama is fond of saying, a "teachable moment." The messianic mission is to perfect mankind in accordance with this "truth." The

---

3. J. L. Talmon, *The Origins of Totalitarian Democracy* (Frederick A. Praeger Publishers, 1960); see also Andrew C. McCarthy, "Future Tense VIII: Enter Totalitarian Democracy" (*The New Criterion*, April 2012).

coercive force of law becomes the totalitarian framework in which "truth" is taught and enforced.

While progressivism grips Western elites, most of the public resists. That is because an exclusive pattern of social existence is not compatible with a liberty culture, in which, if given the freedom to do so, people will make a wide variety of different choices. Nevertheless, this does not dampen the progressive's enthusiasm for imposing his pieties. Nor does the progressive sense that this is inconsistent with democracy: Sure, a disciplined minority may have to cajole, coerce, or even trick the majority into doing the right things, but once the majority sees the benefits of progressive policies it will choose those policies for its own good—or so he says.

You will quickly notice that sharia in an Islamist society serves precisely the function that law serves in totalitarian democracy: It suppresses free expression, free will, and volition. Conformity eventually becomes "free choice" because it is the only available choice. As Talmon put it, addressing the tension between freedom and the progressive vision:

> This difficulty could only be resolved by thinking not in terms of men as they are, but as they were meant to be, and would be, given the proper conditions. In so far as they are at variance with the absolute ideal, they can be ignored, coerced or intimidated into conforming without any real violation of the democratic principle being involved. *In the proper conditions*, it is held, the conflict between spontaneity and duty would disappear, and with it the need for coercion. The practical question is, of course, whether constraint will disappear because all have learned to act in harmony, or *because all opponents have been eliminated*. [emphasis added]

Islam, we are tirelessly reminded by its apologists (citing Sura 2:256), prohibits compulsion in matters of religion. We need, however, to read the sharia fine-print. True, Islam will not force you to become a believer—at least not officially. It has no compunction, however, about imposing what Talmon would call "the proper conditions": the sharia system. In fact, sharia assumes the presence in the caliphate of non-believers, whose subjugation has a sobering *in terrorem* effect (and whose obligatory poll tax promotes the sharia state's fiscal health). The concept is that with enough coercion, there will eventually be no need for coercion: everyone, of his own accord, will come to the good sense of becoming a Muslim—all other alternatives having been dhimmified into desuetude.

Progressives see no problem with the notion of "Islamic democracy," including its sharia framework, because its repressive nature aligns with their own conception of democracy: messianic mission, not the preservation of liberty. It should go without saying that progressives and Islamic supremacists subscribe to very different versions of the "sole and exclusive truth"—although, as I demonstrated in *The Grand Jihad*, this does not prevent their frequent collaborations. Those joint efforts—carefully sidestepping immense differences between progressives and Islamists on freedom of conscience, equality for women and non-Muslims, sexual liberty, and a host of other matters—occur because the two sides see eye-to-eye on many foundational issues. One is that there is no inconsistency between democracy and repression, between "freedom" and punishing those who fail to conform to the "truth."

CHAPTER THREE

Sharia and Factophobia

"From a purely academic point of view, this translation is superior to anything produced by orientalists in the way of translations of major Islamic works." Taha Jabir al-Alwani was writing about *Reliance of the Traveller—A Classic Manual of Islamic Sacred Law.*

The original manual, *Umdat al-Salik*, was meticulously drawn from Muslim scripture by Ahmad ibn Naqib al-Misri, a fourteenth-century sharia scholar. It was not until 1991 that *Reliance*, the first English translation, became available in the United States. That it earned Dr. Alwani's accolades is no small thing. He is a globally recognized authority in *fiqh*—Islamic jurisprudence—having earned a prestigious al-Azhaar University doctorate in the subject.

Alwani's history underscores that, while we justifiably fret over the Muslim Brotherhood's increasing hold on the Middle East, the Brotherhood dominates the development and presentation of Islam in the United States, too—exploiting a government so desperate to "reach out" to Muslims that it is reliably found canoodling with, and thus increasing the cachet of, Islamic supremacists whose defining trait is contempt for the West.

Before relocating to America in the early 1980s, Alwani lived in Saudi Arabia, where he became a prominent member of the World Assembly of Muslim Youth. Founded in 1972, WAMY is a seminal collaboration between Brotherhood theoreticians and the Saudi government. Its aim is to indoctrinate students in Sunni supremacism. As related in one of the organization's pamphlets, "Islam at a Glance," WAMY's animating concept is to "arm the Muslim youth with full confidence in the supremacy of the Islamic system over other systems."

In classic Brotherhood legerdemain, WAMY's promotion of supremacism in the West is veiled by the "inter-faith understanding" charade. In these now familiar rituals, Christian and Jewish clerics explain how much they admire Islam, then Muslim clerics reciprocate by explaining how much they admire Islam. WAMY has described this aspect of its mission as "introduc[ing] Islam to non-Muslims in its purest form as a comprehensive system and way of life." You'll no doubt be stunned to learn that WAMY's American branch was founded by a nephew of the famously ecumenical Osama bin Laden.

In any event, back on Islam's home turf, WAMY has never been very subtle, outlining in a short book called *Islamic Views*—printed by the Saudi government's Armed Forces Printing Press—its goal to "teach our children to love taking revenge on the Jews and the oppressors, and teach them that our youngsters will liberate Palestine and al-Quds [i.e., Jerusalem] when they go back to Islam and make Jihad for the sake of Allah." WAMY, moreover, has been tied by extensive evidence to the financial support of Hamas and al Qaeda.[1] And as we shall see, it was the original breeding ground

---

1.   See, e.g., Matthew Levitt, *Hamas: Politics, Charity, and Terrorism in the Service of Jihad* (Yale University Press, 2006), pp. 116-18, 159, 168-69, 192-94; Steven G. Merley, *Turkey, the Global Muslim Brotherhood, and the Gaza Flotilla* (Jerusalem Center for Public Affairs, 2011), p. 31.

for decades of collaboration between the Muslim Brotherhood and Turkish Islamists, very much including Prime Minister Recep Tayyip Erdogan.

A CALL TO PRAYER FROM THE WORLD TRADE CENTER RUBBLE

In Saudi Arabia, Alwani also taught Islamic law for a decade at one of the regime's prestigious universities and became a member of the Islamic Fiqh Academy. Soon after moving here in 1983, he joined a group of prominent Islamic scholars living in the West to form the Fiqh Council of North America (FCNA), the most prominent sharia body in the United States.

FCNA evolved from the Religious Affairs Committee of the Muslim Students Association (MSA), the Muslim Brotherhood's first toehold in the United States. Just as the MSA eventually spawned the Islamic Society of North America (ISNA), America's largest and most consequential Islamist organization, so did the MSA's Religious Affairs Committee morph into ISNA's Fiqh Committee. In the mid-Eighties, ISNA reconstituted the Fiqh Committee as the FCNA and Alwani became its chairman. Both FCNA and ISNA were among the 29 Islamist organizations Muslim Brotherhood officials identified as "our friends" in their notorious 1991 "Explanatory Memorandum"—the document in which the Brothers declared that their "work in America is a kind of grand Jihad in eliminating and destroying the Western civilization from within."[2]

Dr. Alwani is now president of Cordoba University in Virginia, an academic institution dedicated to Islamic learning as prescribed by the Brotherhood. The school is named after the capital city of the caliphate that conquered Spain in the Middle Ages. By a remarkable coincidence, the project to build a triumphal mosque and Islamic center on the remains of the World Trade Center complex in lower Manhattan was called the "Cordoba Initiative." Small world. Turns

---

2. McCarthy, *The Grand Jihad* pp. 57-60.

out that Feisal Abdul Rauf, the imam behind this "Ground Zero Mosque" project, wrote a book that was originally marketed under the title, *A Call to Prayer from the World Trade Center Rubble: Islamic Dawa in the Heart of America Post-9/11. Dawa* is the proselytism of sharia by means other than violence and agents other than terrorists—the "stealth jihad," as Robert Spencer put it, involving resistance to assimilation, intimidation of critics, cultivation of sympathizers in the media and the universities, exploitation of our legal system and tradition of religious liberty, infiltration of our political system, fundraising, and the portrayal of any scrutiny of Islamic doctrine as "Islamophobia." It is through *dawa* that Sheikh Qaradawi boldly vows, "We will conquer Europe, we will conquer America!"

The Brotherhood liked Imam Rauf's book so much, it arranged for a non-commercial edition to be distributed in the United States in order, as the preface notes explain, "to promote a proper understanding of Islam and common ground between Islam and the West." Yes, of course. Being a Brotherhood venture, the new edition was rebranded in 2004 with the less provocative title, *What's Right with Islam Is What's Right with America.*

In collaboration with ISNA, funding for the new edition was provided by the International Institute of Islamic Thought (IIIT). And it just so happens that when Taha Jabir al-Alwani wrote his endorsement of *Reliance of the Traveller* in 1990, he was acting in his then-capacity as president of IIIT. It, too, is one of the twenty-nine "friends" the Muslim Brotherhood named in its Explanatory Memorandum.

TRUSTEES OF THE MISSION

With the usual combination of Brotherhood know-how and Saudi funding, IIIT was established as an Islamist think-tank in 1980 "to train and prepare Islamic scholars in the field of the Islamization of social sciences and to encourage them to research and write on social science topics from an Islamic perspective." The Hudson Institute's Zeyno Baran correctly surmises that IIIT's stated mission, "the Islamization of knowledge," is a "euphemism for the rewriting of history to support Islamist narratives." Naturally, IIIT's founders are intimately tied to the Brotherhood's infrastructure in the United States, including MSA, ISNA and CAIR (the Council on American-Islamic Relations)—all of whose involvement in what the Brotherhood calls its "civilization jihad" against the West was established at the *Holy Land Foundation* trial, the Justice Department's successful prosecution of several Islamic supremacists for routing millions of dollars to the Brotherhood's Palestinian jihadist branch, Hamas.

During Alwani's tenure, IIIT made a $50,000 contribution to WISE, the World Islamic Study Enterprise, founded by the University of South Florida professor Sami al-Arian. As fate would have it, al-Arian was a top operative of Palestinian Islamic Jihad, another murderous terrorist organization. Not that this dissuaded Alwani, who gushed in a letter that he considered his "honorable brother" al-Arian to be an "extension of" the IIIT and a "trustee of the Mission." The Brotherhood network labored feverishly to denigrate his prosecution as an exercise in paranoia and anti-Muslim bigotry, but al-Arian eventually pled guilty to a terrorism charge. The sentencing judge blasted him as a "master manipulator," adding, "You looked your neighbors in the eyes and said you had nothing to do with the Palestinian Islamic Jihad. This trial exposed that as a lie." The whole al-Arian episode resulted in some embarrassment for Alwani, who was cited by the Justice Department as an unindicted co-conspirator in the case.

This kind of thing is not altogether unusual for Dr. Alwani. You're apt to get mixed up with some regrettable company when you sign on, as he did during the first Intifada, to a sharia experts' fatwa that echoed the Hamas charter by pronouncing that, "Jihad is the only way to liberate Palestine," and that "no person may settle the

Jews on the land of Palestine or cede to them any part thereof, or recognize any right therein for them."[3]

Another embarrassing affiliation turned out to be Abdurahman Alamoudi, one of FCNA's original trustees. Once a celebrated "moderate" in Washington circles, Alamoudi was tapped by the Clinton White House as an "Islamic affairs" adviser and by the State Department as its "goodwill ambassador" to Muslim nations. Wouldn't you know, he turned out to be a financier for al Qaeda and Hezbollah. Alamoudi was arrested in 2003 while transporting $340,000 in cash that he'd received from the Qaddafi regime in Libya to finance an assassination attempt by al Qaeda operatives on then-Crown Prince (now King) Abdullah of Saudi Arabia. It later emerged that the government had recordings of Alamoudi lamenting the dearth of Americans casualties in al Qaeda's 1998 bombing of the American embassy in Kenya—in addition to urging more terrorist attacks against Israeli interests and elaborating on his goal of gradually converting the United States into an Islamic country.

Before Alamoudi was exposed as a jihadist, his friends at the IIIT helped persuade the Clinton Defense Department to select two organizations that would be tasked to certify Muslim chaplains for the U.S. armed forces. One was Alamoudi's American Muslim Armed Forces and Veterans Affairs Council; the other was the Graduate School of Islamic and Social Sciences (GSISS), a division of Alwani's Cordoba University.

Notwithstanding this background, GSISS still has the gig. Nor, apparently, is the Defense Department troubled by a GSISS-issued fatwa that states, "We abide by every law of this country *except those laws that are contradictory to Islamic law.*" In fact, the school, which has been turning out graduates since 1999, is now the educational institution credentialed by the Pentagon for

3. Testimony of Steven Emerson, U.S. House of Representatives Committee on Foreign Affairs, Subcommittee on Terrorism, Nonproliferation, and Trade (July 31, 2008), p. 29 & n. 181.

training imams. That would be the same Pentagon that could not bring itself to utter the words "Islam" or "jihad" in the 80-odd pages of its 2010 report "Protecting the Force," on the lessons to be gleaned from the mass-murder attack at Fort Hood. That atrocity was carried out by Major Nidal Hassan, a five-alarm jihadist who made no secret of his ideology in the years before he finally opened fire on his fellow soldiers, screaming, "Allahu Akbar!" as he killed fourteen and wounded thirty. Although the incident resulted in twice as many deaths as the 1993 World Trade Center bombing, the Defense Department labels it not as terrorism but as a case of "workplace violence."

"THE BOOK WILL BE OF GREAT USE"

But I digress. Or do I? After all, with our government consulting them and "partnering" with them, you are supposed to see outfits like ISNA, FCNA, IIIT, Cordoba University, and GSISS as pro-Western "moderates." Yet, they are run, by and large, not by Muslims born and raised in America, but by transplanted Brotherhood operatives steeped in the Islam of the Middle East. They and their alphabet soup of Islamist organizations are promoted as America's "Muslim leaders," the lens through which you are supposed to see sharia—the "classic" version of Islamic law that holds sway in the Middle East—as a promising framework for what is to be the seamless, U.S.-supported transition from dictatorial oppression to "Islamic democracy."

Therefore, the last thing anyone wants you to do is actually *read the manual*.

Dr. Alwani's lavish praise for *Reliance of the Traveller* was significant enough to be included in the book's preface, in the form of a thoroughgoing IIIT "report" endorsing the manual's rendering of sharia. He described the translation as an "eminent work of Islamic jurisprudence," the purpose of which was to make a faithful interpretation of sharia "accessible" to English speakers who are not fluent in the original Arabic. "The book will be of great use," he elaborated, "in America, Britain, and Canada," among other countries.

Alwani and IIIT were not alone in championing *Reliance*. Plaudits also came in from prominent Islamic organizations in Syria and Jordan. Far more significantly, IIIT's commendation is followed in the manual's preface by a similar certification from no less than the Islamic Research Academy at al-Azhar University in Cairo. "We certify," the famed scholars wrote, that the "translation corresponds to the Arabic original and conforms to the practice and faith of the orthodox Sunni Community. . . . There is no objection to printing it and circulating it. . . . May Allah give you success in serving Sacred Knowledge and the religion." There could be no more coveted stamp of scholarly approval in Islam.

But then we move from the endorsements to the manual itself. It is, to say the least, startling. To take just a few of its innumerable bracing instructions, *Reliance* explains that:

- Apostasy from Islam is "the ugliest form of unbelief" for which the penalty is death ("When a person who has reached puberty and is sane voluntarily apostatizes from Islam, he deserves to be killed"). (*Reliance* o8.0 & ff.)
- Apostasy occurs not only when a Muslim renounces Islam but also, among other things, when a Muslim appears to worship an idol, when he is heard "to speak words that imply unbelief," when he makes statements that appear to deny or revile Allah or the prophet Mohammed, when he is heard "to deny the obligatory character of something which by consensus of Muslims is part of Islam," and when he is heard "to be sarcastic about any ruling of the Sacred Law." (*Reliance* o8.7; see also p9.0 & ff.)
- "Jihad means to war against non-Muslims." (*Reliance* o9.0.)

- It is an annual requirement to donate a portion of one's income to the betterment of the ummah (an obligation called *zakat*, which is usually, and inaccurately, translated as "charity"—*zakat* can only be given to Muslims and is designed strictly to fortify the Muslim community, not benefit the less fortunate generally); of this annual donation, one-eighth must be given to "*those fighting for Allah*, meaning people engaged in Islamic military operations for whom no salary has been allotted in the army roster. . . . They are given enough to suffice them for the operation even if they are affluent; of weapons, mounts, clothing and expenses." (*Reliance*, h8.1-17.)
- Non-Muslims are permitted to live in an Islamic state only if they follow the rules of Islam, pay the non-Muslim poll tax, and comply with various adhesive conditions designed to remind them that they have been subdued, such as wearing distinctive clothing, keeping to one side of the street, not being greeted with "Peace be with you" ("*as-Salamu alaykum*"), not being permitted to build as high as or higher than Muslims, and being forbidden to build new churches, recite prayers aloud, "or make public displays of their funerals or feast-days." (*Reliance* o11.0 & ff.)
- Offenses committed against Muslims, including murder, are more serious than offenses committed against non-Muslims. (*Reliance* o1.0 & ff; p2.0-1.)
- The penalty for spying against Muslims is death. (*Reliance* p50.0 & ff; p.74.0& ff.)
- The penalty for fornication is to be stoned to death, unless one is without the "capacity to remain chaste," in which case the penalty is "being scourged one hundred stripes and banished to a distance of at least 81 km./50mi. for one year." (*Reliance* o12.0 & ff.)

- The penalty for homosexual activity ("sodomy and lesbianism") is death. (*Reliance* p17.0 & ff.)
- A Muslim woman may only marry a Muslim man; a Muslim man may marry up to four women, who may be Muslim, Christian, or Jewish (but no apostates from Islam). (*Reliance* m6.0 & ff.—Marriage.)
- A woman is required to be obedient to her husband and is prohibited from leaving the marital home without permission; if permitted to go out, she must conceal her figure or alter it "to a form unlikely to draw looks from men or attract them." (*Reliance* p42.0 & ff.)
- A non-Muslim may not be awarded custody of a Muslim child. (*Reliance* m13.2-3.)
- A woman has no right of custody of her child from a previous marriage when she remarries "because married life will occupy her with fulfilling the rights of her husband and prevent her from tending to the child." (*Reliance* m13.4.)
- The penalty for theft is amputation of the right hand. (*Reliance* o14.0.)
- The penalty for drinking alcohol is "to be scourged forty stripes." (*Reliance* o16.3; p.14.2.)
- The penalty for accepting interest ("usurious gain") is death (i.e., to be considered in a state of war against Allah). (*Reliance* p7.0 & ff.)
- It is forbidden to make pictures of "animate life," for doing so "imitates the creative act of Allah Most High"; "Whoever makes a picture, Allah shall torture him with it on the Day of Judgment until he can breathe life into it, and he will never be able to." (Reliance w50.0 & ff.)
- "Musical instruments of all types are unlawful." Singing is generally prohibited (for "song makes hypocrisy grow in the heart as water does herbage"), and "On the Day of Resurrection Allah will pour molten lead into the ears of whoever

sits listening to a songstress." If they are unaccompanied by musical instruments, however, song and poetry drawn from Islamic scripture and encouraging obedience to Allah are permissible. Ironically, although music is generally forbidden, dancing is permissible "unless it is languid, like the movements of the effeminate." (*Reliance* r40.0 &ff.)

- The testimony of a woman is worth half that of a man. (*Reliance* o24.7.)
- If a case involves an allegation of fornication (including rape), "then it requires four male witnesses." (*Reliance* o24.9.)
- The establishment of a caliphate is obligatory, and the caliph must be Muslim and male. "The Prophet . . . said, "Men are already destroyed when they obey women." (Reliance o25.0 & ff; see also p28.0, on Mohammed's condemnation of "masculine women and effeminate men.")

Again, that's just a sampling. For perusing it or, heaven forfend, for actually cracking open *Reliance of the Traveller* (which is available from Amazon and other booksellers), you're violating a norm and in danger of being smeared as a hater. For writing this easily verifiable summary of a Muslim Brotherhood-endorsed, al-Azhar-recommended sharia treatise, I am an Islamophobe—hysterical, anti-Muslim, etc. That is the template. The ruling class preference is that we, like they, remain willfully blind.

"Islamophobia," however, is not real. It is a neologism contrived by the Brotherhood and adopted by the American Left's grievance industry to taint, as "irrational," entirely rational concerns about an ideology that broadly inspires anti-Western animus and, in a not inconsiderable number of Muslims, violence.

What is real is factophobia, the irrational fear of grappling with the reality of this ideology, of acknowledging the happenstance that Islamic supremacism undergirds the mainstream Islam of the Middle East.

In America, as in Canada and parts of Europe, ambitious, patriotic Muslim reformers struggle—against the government's dumbfounding propensity to empower Islamic supremacists—to preach a very different sharia, one that breaks the tenth-century chains, one that elevates rationalism and the division of the spiritual and civil spheres over Islamist totalitarianism. We can wish them well and support their uphill battle. We cannot, however, confuse our hopes with our reality. The sharia of *Reliance* is the sharia of the Middle East. It cannot coexist with authentic democracy.

CHAPTER FOUR

Pangloss and Pandora

Legend has it that the Arab Spring spontaneously combusted when Mohamed Bouazizi, a fruit vendor, set himself ablaze outside the offices of the Tunisian klepto-cops who had seized his wares. This suicide protest, ignited a sweeping revolt against the corruption and caprices of Arab despots by repressed populations desperate to determine their own destinies. It catalyzed an entire region teeming with young, tech-savvy, secular democrats—latter day Jamal al-Madisons, armed with iPhones and networked by Facebook and Twitter. One by one, the dominoes began to fall: Tunisia, Egypt, Yemen, Libya—joining the shining examples of Afghanistan and Iraq, with adumbral tremors in Saudi Arabia, Jordan, and Bahrain, to say nothing of teetering Syria and rickety Iran. The mass uprising, so the fable goes, is an unmistakable manifestation of what George W. Bush called the "desire for freedom" that "resides in every human heart."

To be sure, President Bush's steely resolve in treating jihadist terror as warfare—rather than as the crime-wave progressives imagined they could subpoena into submission—yielded spectacular national security dividends: the decimation of al Qaeda's operational cells, the copious gathering of life-saving intelligence, and a decade free of jihadist attacks against the homeland. Tragically, though, Mr. Bush was equally instrumental in blinding Americans to the doctrinal underpinnings of Islamic supremacism.

Contrary to Bush's mulish insistence, echoing Bill Clinton and presaging Barack Obama, this doctrine was not hallucinated into existence by the fervid passions of Islamic terrorists or the irrational fears of Western "Islamophobes." It is a central, undeniable component of the Koran, the hadith, and the sacralized biographies of Mohammed—the sacred scriptures of a belief system the precise cause of whose spread was military conquest. Not for nothing did we (in Chapter 1) hear the now-premier of Turkey, last bastion of the caliphate, meld Islamic iconography with the imagery of armed combat: "The mosques are our barracks, the minarets our bayonets, the cupolas our helmets and the faithful our soldiers."

A CONCEPTUAL OXYMORON

As I recounted in *The Grand Jihad*, Hassan al-Banna preached that "it is the nature of Islam to dominate, not to be dominated." The mission of Islam, the Brotherhood's founder elaborated, is "to impose its law on all nations and to extend its power to the entire planet." Banna did not make that up. It is the same thing Tripoli's envoy to London told U.S. emissaries John Adams and Thomas Jefferson over two centuries ago, when they asked him why the Barbary Pirates attacked American ships, took their crews as slaves, and extorted ransoms. The Koran and the "Laws of the Prophet" held that all nations refusing to submit to their authority "were sinners," the envoy explained. Thus, it was the "right and duty" of Muslims "to make war upon them." For fourteen centuries, spreading the doctrine, by hook or by crook, has been Islam's principal calling. Believers take it to be a divine command.

The doctrine fuels violent jihad every bit as much as it inspires non-violent strategems for implementing sharia—such as co-opting democratic processes. One need not agree that this summons to conquest is the only way, or the best way, to interpret Islamic doctrine in order to acknowledge, with as much chagrin as candor, that the Islamist interpretation is more than colorable. That would be true even if Islamic supremacism were not regnant among Islam's most influential scholars.

Bush delivered his ode to the purportedly universal craving for liberty in the second inaugural address. This was January 2005, shortly after American forces made quick work, first, of Osama bin Laden's Afghan safe-haven, and next, of two monstrous regimes: the Afghan Taliban and Saddam Hussein's Iraqi Baathists. Crushing America's enemies was not enough, the president decided.

His recipe, the Islamic Democracy Project, is a half-baked mixture of "compassion" (i.e., what passes as conservatism for progressive Republicans) and an epic miscalculation of self-interest—to wit, the loftily harebrained idea that "the survival of liberty in our land increasingly depends on the success of liberty in other lands." Thousands of lives and nearly a trillion dollars later, what have we to show for it? A pair of sharia states hostile to American interests (Iraq is an Iranian satellite; Afghanistan verges on a Taliban re-conquest), to go along with a regional cavalcade of jihadists and totalitarian Islamists, now swaddled in sovereign legitimacy thanks to the subordination of democratic *culture* to democratic *procedures*—as if electing a class president somehow made the third grade a "democracy" and the schoolyard bullies a "political party."

Back in the heady days of the second Bush inaugural, Islamic democracy was still a Panglossian dream, not the Pandora's box it became once Islamist parties began to win elections with regularity. Even then, it was palpable that "Islamic democracy" was a conceptual oxymoron: having, in practice, everything to do with Islam and

41

precious little to do with Western democracy. Let's put aside for now the case of Turkey, a pre-existing democracy whose Islamists, upon achieving power, made like termites, gradually destroying the democratic framework from within. Let's consider, instead, a "Made in the U.S.A." gambit to erect an Islamic democracy from scratch in a country with a nearly 100 percent Muslim population.

Here's a riddle: What begins with words "In the Name of God, the Merciful, the Compassionate," a formal Islamic salutation also commonly used by jihadists in their warnings, fatwas, and post-atrocity claims of responsibility? What extols the virtues of "rightful jehad" (also known as *jihad*) in its very first sentence?

What in its first article declares a sovereign "Islamic Republic," and in its second installs Islam as the official "religion of the state"?

What, in its third article announces to the world that, within the territory it governs, "no law can be contrary to the beliefs and provisions of the sacred religion of Islam"?

What sets the national calendar by Mohammed's historic journeys, requires the promotion of religious education, and even mandates that its national anthem must contain the supremacist battle cry "*Allahu Akbar*"?

What calls for that same battle cry to be grafted onto its national flag, along with "the sacred phrase of 'There is no God but Allah and Mohammad is His prophet'"?

What dictates, in the formation of families and upbringing of children, the "elimination of traditions contrary to the principles of [the] sacred religion of Islam"?

What requires the nation's president to be a Muslim, and to swear to Allah, at the beginning of the oath of office, "to obey and safeguard the provisions of the sacred religion of Islam"? What similarly demands this oath of all public ministers?

What permits its judges, in lieu of any civil legal training, to be schooled in Islamic jurisprudence? What decrees that, upon assuming their offices, those judges take an oath "to support justice and righteousness in accord with the provisions of the sacred religion of Islam"?

What enables its highest court, even if predominantly comprised of judges trained only in Islamic law, to interpret for all departments of government the meaning of any law or treaty?

What requires, when no other law directly applies to a question, that the courts resolve it "in accord with the *Hanafi* jurisprudence" (Hanafi being one of the four major schools of Sunni Islamic law), with the lone exception that Shia Islamic principles can be applied in legal cases exclusively involving Shiite Muslims?

What permits any of its terms to be altered with the sole exception that "The provisions of adherence to the fundamentals of the sacred religion of Islam and the regime of the Islamic Republic cannot be amended"?

You win the prize if you answered: the new constitution of Afghanistan, entered into force on January 4, 2004, with the giddy approval of the U.S Department of State.

"FREEDOM" EQUALS THE "PERFECT SLAVERY"

Ambassador Zalmay Khalilzad, President Bush's emissary to Afghanistan, who would later bring this same magic touch to Iraq, cooed at the time that the new constitution set forth "parallel commitments to Islam and to human rights." This was gobbledy diplo-speak. If by "parallel," Dr. Khalilzad meant there were a few sonorous human-rights tropes in the document, then sure: there were enough to camouflage, at least for a while, the embarrassing fact that the Taliban itself could have ruled quite comfortably under the constitution's terms. But if one takes "parallel" in common parlance, as connoting a sense of roughly equal deference to Islamic law and to human rights, the State Department was deluding itself—or, at least, deluding the rest of us.

The Afghans were not fooled, though. Before long, they made it crystal clear that, in reality, "Islamic democracy" is simply the establishment of sharia repression by referendum rather than force of arms. Abdul Rahman, a Christian who had converted from Islam years earlier, was imprisoned and put on trial for the *capital offense* of apostasy.

This was a surprise to exactly no one versed in both the new Afghan constitution and classical sharia: the former elevates the latter, and, as we've seen, the latter plainly prescribes the death penalty for those who renounce Islam.

This injunction is so firmly rooted in scripture that it is the subject of consensus across the four major Islamic jurisprudential traditions. The Koran's sura 4:89, for example, states: "They would have you disbelieve as they themselves have disbelieved, so that you may all be alike. Do not befriend them until they have fled their homes for the cause of Allah. *If they desert you, seize them and put them to death wherever you find them.* Look for neither friends nor helpers among them." Mind you, Koranic passages are taken by believers to be the words of Allah himself.

Muslims, moreover, are taught to revere and emulate the prophet, whose thoughts on the matter of apostasy are recorded in authoritative hadiths, such as: "A Muslim . . . may not be killed except for three reasons: as punishment for murder, for adultery, or for apostasy" (Bukhari collection, No. 9.83.17); and "Whoever changes his Islamic religion, then kill him" (Bukhari No. 9.84.57). That is fairly straightforward, wouldn't you say? Consequently, mainstream Islamic scholarship holds that apostasy, certainly once it is publicly revealed, warrants the death penalty. That a handful of Western academics and duplicitous Islamists appear to think they can cleverly rationalize their way around this consensus has, it bears reiterating, no relevance to Islam as it is lived in the Muslim Middle East.

If the stakes were not life and death, or if the United States had not sacrificed blood and treasure only to find Islam's draconian sharia installed as foundational law, it might have been amusing to watch State Department officials and European ministers wring their hands as if there had been some terrible misunderstanding—as if someone in Afghanistan's sharia-steeped judiciary must have forgotten that, as a U.S. government spokesman spluttered, "freedom of worship [and] freedom of expression . . . are bedrock principles of democracy . . . that are enshrined in the Afghan constitution."

Alas, there is nothing amusing about a tragic truth to which we remain willfully blind: "Freedom" in an Islamic society is not liberty; it is submission to sharia—"perfect slavery," as the renowned "Sufi Master" Ibn Arabi expressed the concept in the thirteenth century.[1] As Andrew Bostom recounts, the eleventh-century Sufi scholar known as al-Qushayri elaborated on this distinction:

> Let it be known to you that the real meaning of freedom lies in the perfection of slavery. If the slavery of a human being in relation to God is a true one, his freedom is relieved from the yoke of changes. Anyone who imagines that it may be granted to a human being to give up his slavery for a moment and disregard the commands and prohibitions of the religious law while possessing discretion and responsibility has divested himself of Islam.

Professor Bernard Lewis reaffirmed this understanding of *hurriya* (the arabic word for "freedom") in a mid-Twentieth Century contribution to the *Encyclopedia of Islam* (2d edition), describing life in the last gasps of the Ottoman Empire:

> [T]here is still no idea that the subjects have any right to share in the formation or conduct of government—to political freedom, or citizenship, in the sense which underlies the development of political thought in the West. While conservative reformers

---

1. Andrew G. Bostom, "Contra Bush 43, Most Americans Aware Muslim World in No Hurr(i)y(ya) for Real Reform" (AndrewBostom.org May 16, 2012); Franz Rosenthal, *The Muslim Concept of Freedom* (Leiden, Brill 1960).

talked of freedom under law, and some Muslim rulers even
experimented with councils and assemblies, government was in
fact becoming more and not less arbitrary

In fact, while one risks being banished from polite society for pointing
this out today, Lewis added that individual liberty in Islamic countries "was on the whole more extensive and better protected" during
the period of colonial domination by the British and French "than
either before or after." It has been no different in modern times:
It was Mubarak's military regime in Egypt that outlawed practices
like female genital mutilation; it was Musharaff's military regime in
Pakistan that outlawed such sharia cruelties as forced marriage and
stoning.

Even if we grant for argument's sake the dubious Bushian proposition that all human beings crave freedom, Islam and the West have
never seen eye-to-eye about what "freedom" means. Consequently,
to sell "Islamic democracy" as a quest for freedom is to sell snake oil.

Freedom of conscience is embedded in liberty's irreducible core.
Yet the concept is alien to Muslim societies and, hence, to "Islamic
democracy." Even if that proposition were not obvious to those
who have studied Middle Eastern norms (however ignorant of it
Americans have remained), Afghanistan's constitutional text removes
all doubt. Regardless of the frilly "human rights" ornamentation
included in the document, it emphatically commands: *No law can
be contrary to the beliefs and provisions of the sacred religion of Islam.*

With some arm-twisting of Hamid Kharzai, the duplicitous
Afghan president with whom it is our lot to be stuck, Abdul Rahman
was quietly whisked out of the country before the death sentence
could be executed. For this Afghan, "Islamic democracy" was a dun-
geon, not a safe harbor. The oldest lie in the book was used to justify
his extradition: the defendant was pronounced *non compos mentis*—
after all, what else could possibly explain a desire to convert from
Islam?

ISLAMIC CONSTITUTIONAL RIGHTS

This embarrassing misadventure led to exactly zero movement to repeal the apostasy law. Quite the contrary: the sharia standard was invoked yet again five years later, when Said Musa, an Afghan Red Cross worker, was locked up for becoming a Christian. Again under intense pressure from crimson-faced champions of "Islamic democracy," Karzai allowed the prisoner to be ushered out of Afghanistan—even though Musa declined the unrepentant regime's request that he publicly express regret over his conversion.

"Islamic democracy" turned out not to be very democratic for him, either. It is nothing short of abominable that its architects suggest otherwise, particularly given the enterprise's record of persecuting minority religions (see Chapter 2). That record, one might add, was as foreseeable as it is appalling: of the fifty nations most notorious for persecuting Christians, thirty-eight are Islamic, according to the Open Doors organization's 2011 World Watch List.

Nor is "Islamic democracy" much of a boon for women. At the end of 2011, Karzai's office announced that the president had magnanimously commuted the prison sentence of a nineteen-year-old woman who was serving a twelve-year term imposed by an Afghan court after she was convicted of . . . having sex out of wedlock . . . *with a relative who had raped her.* Karzai's rationale for the pardon? The woman had cured her indiscretion by agreeing to marry the rapist, whose child she had borne during her jail term. In reporting the story, the Associated Press noted in passing that "about half of the 300 to 400 women jailed in Afghanistan are imprisoned for so-called 'moral crimes' such as sex outside marriage, or running away from their husbands."

Then there's Iraq. As we've seen, since adopting its "democratic" constitution in 2005, Iraq has earned the distinction of becoming one of the world's most "systematic" and "egregious" violators of religious liberty. And, the U.S. Commission on International Religious Freedom adds, things are getting steadily worse. "Despite an overall decrease in violence in the country," the Commission wrote in a late 2011 letter to President Obama, "members of Iraq's smallest religious minorities, including Christians, Sabean Mandaeans, and Yazidis continue to suffer from targeted violence, threats and intimidation."

The commissioners pleaded with the president to raise the matter publicly with Nouri al-Maliki, Iraq's prime minister (who now clings to power despite losing the last democratic election). Obama, plainly more embarrassed by the Commission than by Iraq's Islamist regime, demurred. The president preferred to prattle about "a new Iraq that's determining its own destiny—a country in which people from different religious sects and ethnicities resolve their differences peacefully through the democratic process."

Well, not exactly.

Under American guidance, the new Iraqi constitution, like its Afghan forerunner, established Islam as the state religion and installed sharia as "a main source for legislation." Blinkered devotees of the Islamic Democracy Project celebrated this as dexterous craftsmanship, as if the phrase "*a* main source" was sure to be seen as crucially different from "*the* main source" once the sharia judges got their mitts on it.

Those of us who scrutinized the document, rather than just listening to the knee-jerk applause, found that it "guarantees the Islamic identity of the majority of the Iraqi people"—so that even if a majority someday wished a non-Islamic or secular identity (I know, I know: fat chance), their constitution would forbid such a free choice. Furthermore, the constitution enables sharia experts to occupy a majority of the seats on Iraq's highest court, and makes that court responsible for "[s]upervising the legitimacy" of all laws—both before and after they are enacted.

For a true democrat, that would seem less than reassuring, particularly when the constitution is considered against the backdrop of Iraqi society. In large numbers, Iraqis elected Shiite political parties closely tied to Iran's revolutionary Islamic government—parties that would, given their druthers, impose a Shiite sharia state. Equally disheartening: to entice public support for its Iraqi "democracy" initiative, the Bush administration courted Iraq's revered Islamic jurist, Ayatollah Ali al-Sistani.

This courting had to be done from a distance. As we've seen, Sistani does not mingle with non-Muslims and counsels the faithful to avoid touching them. In fact, as the former Reagan official John Agresto observed, Sistani is "an open anti-Semite and a not-too-subtle anti-Christian," who is "bent on establishing a theocracy not far removed from that found in Iran." The word he uses in referring to non-Muslims is *kafir*. To say, dictionary-style, that this term means "infidel" or "non-Muslim" would not quite do justice to Sistani's views. At the website on which he instructs the faithful on the principles of Islam, here is the guidance he published in 2006 (before said guidance was yanked when us hysterical Islamophobes called attention to it):

> *Kafir*: An infidel, i.e. a person who does not believe in Allah and His Oneness, is *najis* [filth]. . . . And similar is the case of those who deny Prophethood, or any of the necessary laws of Islam[.] As regards the people of the Book (i.e. the Jews and the Christians) who do not accept the Prophethood of Prophet Muhammad bin Abdullah (Peace be upon him and his progeny), they are commonly considered *najis* [i.e., filth], but it is not improbable that they are *Pak*. [*Pak* is defined as clean, the opposite of *najis*] However, it is better to avoid them. . . . The entire body of a Kafir, including his hair and nails, and all liquid substances of his body, are *najis*. . . .

Well, it's good to have democratic allies.

CHAPTER FIVE

They Just Don't Like Us

Like its successor, the Bush administration discouraged all inquiry into Islamic doctrine by anyone seeking to understand Muslim enmity. It simultaneously indulged two mutually exclusive delusions: (a) that as a "religion of peace," Islam is one of America's best strategic assets in the battle against "extremism"; and (b) that the West is capable of cultivating the reform and moderation needed to cure the dysfunction and anguish that pervade Islamic societies.

Inexorably, this has fed President Barack Obama's preferred delusion: Since Islam is both virtuous and filled with contempt for the West, the West must be to blame for Islam's fury. As is his wont, Obama exponentially ratchets up the damage of his predecessor's every "compassionate" distortion. Where Bush airbrushed Muslim supremacists, Obama embraces them. Where Bush retreated from such clarifying terms as *jihad* and *Islamofascism* due to caterwauling from the Brotherhood's American grievance chorus, Obama stridently objects to utterances of the word *Islam* for any purpose other than hagiography—and enthusiastically contributes to the slander that anyone who sees things differently is a hate-mongering "Islamophobe." Indeed, under Obama's guidance, the National Aeronautics and Space Administration's mission devolved from expanding our galactic horizons to inflating the self-esteem of Muslim nations—"to help them feel good about their historic contribution to science," said NASA administrator Charles Bolden, recalling the president's directive.

The flawed assumption underlying both administrations' approaches to what they tellingly call "the Muslim world"—as if the Muslim Middle East and the rest of the ummah were an alien planet, beyond our comprehension—is that Islamic peoples are just like Western peoples; it's just that their aspirations, which are no different from anyone else's, have been crushed under the yoke of colonialism and dictatorship. That Islam simply is a fundamentally distinct civilization; that its history diverges from the West's path because its culture and principles proceed from different premises; that it does not emulate the West because it fervently sees its own mores and values as not only different but superior—these possibilities are never permitted to enter our calculations.

WHAT THEY WANT IS A SHARIA SPRING

In point of fact, the contemporary Muslim indictment against Middle Eastern dictators begins with the charge that they have *repressed Islam*, not that they have *denied individual liberty*. This is not to say that other complaints are irrelevant. Muslims have indeed been outraged by the manner in which their Arafats, Mubaraks, Qaddafis, and Saddams looted the treasuries while the masses lived in squalor. But Brotherhood leaders—some of whom are fabulously wealthy—portray the despots' purloined fortunes, along with other regime hypocrisies, as a pattern of sin *against Allah's law*, not as the inevitable corruptions of absolute power. Absolute power, after all, is what Islamic supremacists are all about. The House of Saud, which has accumulated far more wealth than all the deposed dictators combined (and used no small amount of it to underwrite the Brotherhood and sundry jihadists), continues to enjoy a relatively firm grip on power because it is perceived, for good reason, as the guardian and chief propagator of Islamic supremacist orthodoxy.

It is freely conceded that the Muslims of the Middle East want more say in the matter of choosing their leaders. They certainly prefer the occasional popular election to the flat-out imposition of dictatorship. This, however, is because they seek a more Islamic order, not because they are starving for freedom and self-determination. Elections are not much of a priority once Islamic supremacists take power. In Iraq, for example, Prime Minister Nouri al-Maliki lost the 2010 election but clings to power anyway, resorting to the usual strongman tactics—arresting political adversaries, routing sectarian minorities. Hamas has not permitted another election since it defeated its rival Fatah at the ballot box in late 2006 then savagely routed it in Gaza a few months later.

Neither Maliki nor Hamas is particularly popular among, respectively, Iraqis or Palestinians. Hamas, in fact, is viewed far more favorably by Muslims outside Gaza; they do not know the terrorist organization as their day-to-day ruler, seeing it, instead as the front line against the Zionist enemy—whom Muslims the world over are reared to hate, as my friend Ayaan Hirsi Ali, the intrepid former Muslim, so vividly recounts in her memoir.[1] Nevertheless, if the ruler in an Islamic society is seen as honoring sharia, the ruler is apt to retain power even if the society is not flourishing under his policies. Muslim peoples expect to be ruled, not served, by their leaders. They do not crave the free-wheeling freedom to chart their own destinies; they crave sharia—and in a sharia system, the leader's fidelity is to sharia, not the public.

New Pew polling reaffirms the polling data covered in *The Grand Jihad*, illustrating the strong desire for sharia governance among the

---

1. Ayaan Hirsi Ali, *Nomad—From Islam to America: A Personal Journey Through the Clash of Civilizations* (Free Press, 2011).

Muslims of the Middle East. In 2011, 78 percent of Pakistanis, 70 percent of Jordanians, and 62 percent of Egyptians told pollsters that "laws should strictly follow the teachings of the Koran." To put a finer point on it, the dichotomy in the Middle East is not sharia versus secular democracy; it is exclusive, fully implemented sharia versus the predominance of sharia "principles"—i.e., systems which combine sharia with other law sources (e.g., variations on the Napoleonic Code), making clear that sharia prevails in the event of conflict. In Egypt, for example, while 62 percent want strict sharia, 27 percent would prefer a legal system which, while not strict sharia, "follow[s] the values and principles of Islam." Only 5 percent of respondents said, "laws should not be influenced by the teachings of the Koran." Even in Turkey, where a decade of Erdogan has gradually dismantled an eighty-year secularization effort, only 34 percent eschew Islamic law; a solid majority of 53 percent wants laws that, at the very least, reflect the primacy of sharia principles (45 percent)—with 8 percent calling for strict sharia.

The most influential figures and institutions in Islamic societies are those revered for their mastery of Islamic law and jurisprudence. Most notable today is the Muslim Brotherhood's chief jurist, Sheikh Yusuf al-Qaradawi, an Egyptian scholar notorious for fatwas (sharia edicts) approving suicide terrorism, the murder of American troops in Iraq, and the death penalty for Muslims who publicly apostatize from Islam. Cairo's al-Azhar University remains Islam's ideological Vatican—the academy that has produced such luminaries as Sheikh Qaradawi, Dr. Taha al-Alwani (whom we met in Chapter 3), and Omar Abdel Rahman, the infamous "Blind Sheikh" who inspired the 1993 World Trade Center bombing. It was on Sheikh Abdel Rahman's fatwa calling for the mass-murder of Americans that Osama bin Laden relied in executing the 9/11 atrocities. In the ummah, the Blind Sheikh remains a hero: in the new, post-Mubarak Egypt, demonstrations outside the American embassy demanding his release from U.S. imprisonment, are now routine.

In places where Islam is the central fact of life, even Muslims who privately dismiss sharia take pains to honor it publicly. Even dictatorial regimes in Islamic countries (e.g., Nasserite Egypt, Baathist Iraq, Arafat's Palestinian ministry, Qaddafi's Libya) have appreciated the imperative of paying lip-service to sharia as the backbone of their legal systems. Despots commonly laced their rhetoric with scriptural allusions, and rationalized their actions—though not always convincingly—as Islamically appropriate.

If you understand this, you understand why Western beliefs about the "Arab Spring," and the Western conceit that the death of one tyranny must necessarily herald the birth of liberty, have always been dangerously naive. It was always more likely, in this disparate civilization, that an even more totalitarian form of tyranny would replace the dictators. To be sure, there *are* real democrats throughout the Middle East, authentically moderate Muslims, as well as non-Muslims, who long for freedom in the Western sense. Nevertheless, it is a stubborn fact that they make up a strikingly small fraction of the population: perhaps a hair over 20 percent, a far cry from the Western narrative that posits a sea of Muslim moderates punctuated by the rare radical atoll.

ALLAH IS *GREATER!*

Islamic supremacism is the Middle East mainstream. It is virulently anti-Western, which is why influential Islamic clerics have scoffed at the very notion of Muslim countries' adopting democracy. My argument in this regard—which is really less an *argument* than an *acknowledgment* that Islamic supremacists and their ideas dominate the Middle East—will be twisted by transnational progressives, as if I were saying that Muslims were not "evolved" enough for Western democracies. That, however, is not what I am saying at all.

It is not that Islamists lack the sophistication for democracy. They grasp it as well as we in the West do. They just don't want it. They do not aspire to a culture of liberty. They think their different way of life, based on compliance with what they take to be Allah's beneficent gift of sharia as a framework for virtuous community life, is superior. I do not pretend to be a fan of the Islamists, but how counterproductive it is—for our own security and comprehension of events—to insult their intelligence. It is not that they don't get the West and will come to like us better once they become more familiar with our ways. They understand us just fine. That is why they don't like us.

Go back to the Pew polling for a moment. As the pollsters conclude, "The image of the United States remains overwhelmingly negative in predominantly Muslim countries." This finding is consistent as you move through the populations in the poll, in Egypt, the Palestinian territories, Jordan, Pakistan and Turkey: four out of every five people have an unfavorable view of America. Things, in fact, have gotten marginally worse in the transition from Bush to Obama. After all the "Muslim outreach"; after all the "partnering" with Muslim Brotherhood organizations and pandering to Islamist aspirations, Islamic animus against America has actually gotten somewhat worse in the last three years. The reason is patent for anyone with eyes willing to see. We do not have a problem of understanding or resentment that more information or cooperation will improve. We have a clash of civilizations—a clash in which, for now, one side pushes aggressively forward while the other makes believe it's not happening.

No one who read *The Grand Jihad*, in which I outlined the history, influence, methodology, and goals of the Muslim Brotherhood, could be surprised by the events of the past two years. As it has demonstrated in each "Arab Spring" venue, the Muslim Brotherhood remains the ummah's most significant organization. It still proclaims unabashedly it's ninety-year-old motto: "Allah is our objective. The Prophet is our leader. The Koran is our law. Jihad is our way. Dying in the way of Allah is our highest hope. *Allahu Akbar! Allahu Akbar!*"

The motto's coda is not just rote chanting. *Allahu akbar!*, which also serves as the chillingly familiar exclamation of Muslim terrorists, is commonly translated as "God is greatest!" But that's not exactly right. It literally means, "Allah is *greater*"—the greater God, the mightier, more fearsome power. It is a *comparative*, ubiquitously invoked by a civilization that sees itself surrounded by hostile forces, forever competing for dominance.

Particularly when addressing Arabic audiences, leading Brotherhood figures do little to disguise their abhorrence of perceived enemies: Israel and the West. Furthermore, while the Brotherhood talks a good game about condemning terrorism, especially when speaking to English audiences, it is just that: a game. Put aside the organization's violent history. Put aside Banna's admonition that the Brothers must train for the inevitability of forcible conflict—and the fact that the years long process of becoming a Muslim Brother requires mastery of Banna's teachings. How convincing can the Brotherhood's purported condemnations of terrorism be when Hamas, *a terrorist organization*, is the Brotherhood's Palestinian branch? During the Intifada begun in the late Eighties, providing material support to Hamas was the Brotherhood's highest priority.

Bear in mind that, like the word *freedom*, the word *terrorism* is construed in diametrically opposite ways by Islamists and Westerners. To an Islamist, "terrorism" involves the unjustifiable (under sharia) killing of *Muslims*. Killing non-Muslim enemies is never terrorism, it is "resistance."

To ingratiate themselves with credulous Western leaders, deceptive Islamists will grudgingly—and after no small amount of tooth-pulling and blame-shifting—condemn terrorist attacks against civilian targets (e.g., the World Trade Center) *in the West*. But this is because they rationalize that such indiscriminate violence can and does kill Muslim civilians, too. This is also why, for example, many Islamists condemned al Qaeda's 1998 bombing of the U.S. embassy in Nairobi: It was not the target they had a problem with; it was the fact that in the implementation, scores of Kenyan Muslims were killed while American diplomatic and security personnel emerged largely unscathed. Yet, not only is there no Muslim condemnation of attacks on American military personnel in Islamic countries; these strikes are endorsed by such prominent sharia authorities as Sheikh Qaradawi and members of the al-Azhar faculty.

Similarly, because Islamic supremacists see Jews as historic, incorrigible enemies; because they regard Israel as Muslim land the Jews are "occupying" by force of arms; and because almost all Israelis serve in the Israeli Defense Forces; Islamists are nearly unanimous in their approval of terrorist attacks targeting even Israeli civilian centers. To the Islamist, there is no such thing as an Israeli "civilian"; everyone is a combatant. That is why Islamists, straight-faced, label Israel as a "terrorist state," even though it is the only authentic Middle Eastern democracy, and the one in which Arab Muslim citizens live in true freedom. That is why, perversely, the destruction of Israel—i.e., the destruction of a real democracy—is a unifying ambition of the "Arab Spring."

The Brotherhood has no trouble claiming to be repulsed by "terrorism." The problem is that the Brothers don't mean what you think you hear. Again, they don't judge themselves by your standards. They operate in accordance with the Islamic concepts of *taqiyya* (strategic lying to infidels) and *taqiyya's* close derivative, *tawriya*. As the scholar Raymond Ibrahim explains, *tawriya* is "creative lying": a literal truth by which the speaker deceives a listener he knows to be ignorant of basic facts and assumptions.

A good example would be "Islamic democracy," which is marketed as the "forward march of freedom." In actuality, it is Recep Tayyip Erdogan's "train" to sharia submission.

CHAPTER SIX

"I Am a Servant of Sharia"

"Thank God almighty, I am a servant of sharia." It was 1994, and Recep Tayyip Erdogan was proud to proclaim his Islamist roots in his native Istanbul, where he served as the mayor—or, as he customarily described himself, the city's "imam."

Erdogan's star was rising in Turkey's political firmament, thanks to his mentor, Necmettin Erbaken, trailblazer of the country's modern Islamist politics. In fact, it was as president of the Istanbul Youth Movement, the shock troops of Erbakan's "National Salvation" party, that Erdogan first made his mark. The main vehicle for his renown was a 1974 theatrical production called *Maskomya*. It was both virulently anti-Semitic and, this being Turkey, sadly popular. The prodigy, then twenty years old, not only wrote and directed the play but performed the lead role, as well. As Andrew Bostom recounts, "*Mas-Kom-Ya* was a compound acronym for 'Masons-Communists-*Yahudi*'—the latter meaning 'Jews.'" In Erdogan's telling, the common denominator of these evil, conspiratorial groups was Judaism.

WHERE ISLAM MEETS THE WEST

Turkey is a plenary Muslim country of seventy-four million. Yet, it does not have a plenary Islamic history. It lies on the fault line between East and West. With a rich, unique history, and one foot planted in Europe, the Turks are not an easy fit in the global ummah that Erdogan, now in his third term as Turkey's prime minister, is undertaking to lead. Indeed, the relative success of Turkish society and its growing stature among Muslims, though publicly celebrated by Arabs, is, privately, a bitter pill for them. Historically, Saudis, Egyptians and other Arabs, Islam's *primus inter pares* and notoriously arrogant about their Muslim authenticity, have been wont to look down their noses at the Turks.

The Ottoman legacy to which modern Turkey is heir was, by the empire's demise in World War I, substantially Eurocentric and largely detached from the everyday affairs of the Arab Middle East. Yes, the population has always featured a strong Islamist plurality, traditionally concentrated in the rural areas. Most urban centers, however, have been secular, Euro-minded strongholds—including much of Eastern Thrace, where the Western half of Istanbul is located. And then there are Turkey's ethnic minorities, most notably the contentious, largely unassimilated Kurds.

This is not to say that Arab countries are strangers to ethnic and sectarian diversity. As we've seen, they feature varying Islamic sects and non-Muslim minorities. They tend, though, to be much more attitudinally homogenous, especially in their animus toward the West. Kemalist Turkey, by contrast, saw itself as part of Europe and its future inclined toward the West. The majority of Kemalists continued to identify themselves as Muslims, but Kemalist cultural secularism bred an indifference to Islamic doctrine's supremacist injunctions and an outright hostility to its sharia framework for society. We should pause, then, to consider how remarkable is the advance of Islamic supremacism in Turkey under Erdogan's cunning stewardship. Comparatively speaking, the Islamist march through the Middle East is sure to be much smoother.

Ataturk's secularization project, repressive of Islamic doctrine and unabashedly hostile to public displays of Islamic culture, could only have happened in Turkey. This is not to suggest that it was a mean feat to muffle Islam in a nearly 100 percent Muslim country where tens of millions of the citizens are Islamists. In fact, a herculean effort was required—and even with that, the project ultimately failed: Erdogan & Co. needed far less time to revert Turkey to the Islamist camp than the Kemalists took to secularize it.

The point is that Ataturk's temporary achievement could never have happened in "one of the Arab Spring countries" (as even al Qaeda emir Ayman al-Zawahiri has fondly taken to calling them). So inscribed is Islam on the DNA of Arab lands that strongmen from Nasser to Arafat to Saddam, despite their secular inclinations, always appreciated the imperative of paying at least lip-service veneration to Islam—and of ostensibly pursuing their agendas within the Islamic framework, not against it—and certainly not by supplanting it.

So how did Erdogan pull off his Islamist coup and provide what is now a template for the "Arab Spring"? He followed the Muslim Brotherhood playbook, a how-to manual for weak but shrewd minorities seeking to strengthen their hands. He was also extraordinarily fortunate in both the self-defeating disarray of his domestic adversaries and the flat-footed fecklessness of his Western admirers. Prominently included among the latter are Bush and Obama administration officials, who have lauded him as a "democrat" while he has dismantled Western democracy, piece by piece.

DEMOGRAPHY VERSUS THE DEEP STATE

The illusion of "Islamic democracy" substitutes a value-neutral procedural shell, the popular election, for the rich substance of democratic culture. Thus demography, so crucial to the recent electoral success of Turkey's Islamists, merits scrutiny.

As Tel-Aviv University's Ehud Toledano explains, the last fifteen years have witnessed a transformative population shift. Whereas three-quarters of Turks used to live in small towns and villages, with the remaining 25 percent in the urban centers, that ratio has reversed. Not only has this urbanization process increased the access of formerly rural Turks to higher education and the global economy; it has meant these more devout Muslims have dramatically impacted the cities with what Toledano calls "their traditional culture and sensitivities."

I more bluntly outlined the phenomenon in *The Grand Jihad*. When Islamists relocate, they change their new surroundings much more than their new surroundings change them. In accordance with Brotherhood jurist Yusuf Qaradawi's "voluntary apartheid" approach, Islamists purposely resettle in enclaves where Muslim self-awareness and sharia hold sway. In light of this strategy's effectiveness in Islamizing swaths of the non-Muslim West, it is no surprise to find it working quite well in Turkey, especially given the Islamist parties' gradual erosion of Kemalist obstacles to Islamization. It is not a coincidence that the electoral success of Islamist parties—beginning with Necmettin Erbakan's election as modern Turkey's first Islamist prime minister in 1996—exactly tracks Turkey's demographic sea-change.

Erdogan's victory formula coupled this enhanced Islamist political consolidation and participation with the peculiarities of Turkey's electoral system. The latter, ironically, were designed to keep Islamsts *out of* power.

When Turkey began permitting multi-party politics after World War II, it rigged the electoral system: declining parliamentary representation to political parties that fail to draw a threshold percentage of the popular vote (today, ten percent). Through the latter half of the twentieth century, this generally meant that the hardcore minority of Islamists could never form a parliamentary majority: A majority of Turks, theoretically reprogrammed by decades of Kemalist secularism, would reliably unite, at least enough to keep the Islamists at bay. But in 2002, the several non-Islamist parties did the unthinkable: they splintered.

This Kemalist implosion seemed inconceivable. Not only were secular factions, right and left, fully cognizant that failure on their part to coalesce was the minority Islamists' only path to power. A splintering had, in fact, very recently happened, with sharp consequences. In December 1995, the Islamist *Refah* (Welfare) Party, founded on the Muslim Brotherhood model by Erbakan in 1983, had managed to win the parliamentary election with only 21 percent of the vote.

So dismayed was Turkey's ruling class, the "deep state," that Erbakan's elevation to the office of prime minister was short-lived. The "deep state" is an elite inner sanctum of top army, government, and judicial officials that has historically served as the decisive bulwark against ever-thrumming Islamic supremacism. Its traditionally steely spine, the Turkish military, is the official guardian of the secular order under the Kemalist constitution. The military staged *coups d'etat* in 1960, 1971, and 1980 when civilian leaders seemed poised to move the nation away from Ataturk's secular vision. In 1997, Erbakan's Islamist surge stirred the deep state yet again.

The generals toppled the new prime minister's governing coalition. The episode is known as the "Postmodern Coup" because the army took pains to resist dissolving Parliament and assuming power directly. Still, the junta did round up a number of notorious Islamist rabble-rousers, including Recep Tayyip Erdogan.

Kemal al-Helbawy, a United Kingdom-based Muslim Brotherhood official, has recounted that the Brotherhood "always had ties with the Islamic movement . . . in Turkey, since its inception"— dating back to Islamist groups Erbakan formed even before he started the National Salvation Party in the Seventies.[1] Erdogan was elected chairman of the NSP's youth corps (the Istanbul Youth Organization) in 1976, not long after his Maskomya star turn. Helbawy, a contemporary, was one of the original leaders of WAMY—the World Assembly of Muslim Youth, the font of Sunni supremacist ideology and terror facilitation that we discussed (in Chapter 3) in connection with another of its alumni, the sharia scholar Taha al-Alwani. According to Helbawy, it was at WAMY, which was active in Turkey as it is in dozens of countries, that he first met Erdogan and several other up-and-coming young Islamists.

When the NSP was closed down by the 1980 military coup, Erdogan followed Erbakan to the new Refah Party, described by Soner Cagaptay, a stellar scholar of Turkey, as "an explicitly Islamist party, which featured strong anti-Western, anti-Semitic, anti-democratic, and anti-secular elements." Erdogan was in his mid-thirties and a leading Refah figure by the time of the Postmodern Coup, during which the deep state, through the instrument of Turkey's constitutional court, banned Refah and other Islamist parties. Erdogan himself was arrested for religious incitement, convicted in 1998, and imprisoned for six months.

THE TURKISH SPRING

It was from the ruins of the banned parties that Erdogan, with the help of his fellow Erbakan acolyte, Abdullah Gul, constructed the AKP (the Justice and Development Party, *Adalet ve Kalkinma Partisi*). The founders' hard experience also induced them to adopt the pragmatic radicalism turned into an art form by the Muslim Brotherhood: softening their supremacist rhetoric while in a position of relative weakness; going the extra mile to appear unthreatening; lying about their true intentions, particularly to a credulous West

---

1. Merley, *Turkey, the Global Muslim Brotherhood, and the Gaza Flotilla*, p. 31 & n. 43.

that is manic to prove its Islamophilia; prioritizing the enhancement of their influence over major societal institutions; directing demagoguery at lighting-rod targets (in Turkey, Jews and Israel work well) in order to rally support; and infiltrating their political opposition, gradually defanging it from within.

As I contended in *The Grand Jihad*, the parallels between the Brotherhood's modus operandi and Saul Alinksy-style ground-up radicalism—also known as "community organizing"—are palpable. They do much to explain the confederation of Islamists and Leftists against the culture of liberty. When both Brotherhood operatives and community organizers speak publicly, they emphasize semiotics over bombast, code words being a perspicacious device for winking in solidarity at one's allies while steering clear of explicit, actionable incitement. In the AKP's case, the choice to name itself after "Justice" speaks volumes.

Hearing the word, ordinary Westerners draw the common inference of simple "fairness" or "rectitude." It seems aspirational, not provocative. But just as the term "social justice" in Leftist parlance connotes an entire system of statism, confiscatory taxation, and redistribution of wealth, Islamist odes to "justice" connote sharia, Islam's legal system and totalitarian societal scheme. It is not for nothing that one of the Brotherhood theorist Sayyid Qutb's most influential tracts is entitled *Social Justice in Islam*—and would be equally at home at either the book-stand of an Occupy Wall Street encampment or an Arab Spring rally.

By 2002, the scene was set for a "Turkish Spring." The multiple Kemalist parties were widely disdained, being seen as sclerotic and responsible for thoroughgoing governmental corruption. Erdogan's Justice and Development Party saw its opening. The AKP pols shrewdly packaged themselves not as implacable Islamists but as pragmatic reformers: members of a conventional, moderate, "socially conservative" movement committed to "improving" the secular framework, not tearing it asunder. Riding the demographic wave, AKP took 34 percent of the vote—nearly doubling Erbakan's haul only seven years earlier. And thus did the purported safeguards Kemalists built into Turkey's electoral system come back to bite the designers: with the wretched showing of the secular parties, the AKP's mere one-third of the vote translated into a stranglehold two-thirds' majority in Parliament.

Michael Rubin, the American Enterprise Institute scholar who has written with singular clarity on Erbakan's Turkey, recounted the debacle in *National Review*. In triumph, Erdogan was sagely subdued. "We are the guardians of this secularism," he feigned, "and our management will clearly prove that." As is reliably the case when Erdogan bats his eyes Westward, there was an ulterior motive. Having been convicted of sedition, he was disqualified from public office. Regardless of his unquestioned control of the AKP, Erdogan was thus denied the premiership he so coveted.

So, while disarming wary onlookers with the AKP's apparent eagerness to please, Erdogan busied himself behind the scenes, arranging to have the prime minister's chair kept warm for him by Gul, fresh from a lengthy stint as a sharia-finance specialist at the Islamic Development Bank in Saudi Arabia—a venerable underwriter of Islamist causes, which, during Gul's IDB tenure, included the Islamization of Sudan.[2] With Gul's leadership and the AKP's stranglehold on Parliament, the law was amended so that Erdogan could run for office. He promptly prevailed in a suspect special election—as Rubin notes, "after a court conveniently threw out the results in one district."

Now officially a member of the legislature, Erdogan became prime minister on March 14, 2003.

2.   Merley, *Turkey, the Global Muslim Brotherhood, and the Gaza Flotilla*, p. 36 & n. 82.

CHAPTER SEVEN

The School of Hard Knocks

One cannot overstate the importance of the lessons Erdogan and the AKP derived from 1997's fleeting rise and fall of the Islamists. It was a school of hard knocks, the pain of Erbakan's abrupt ouster and Erdogan's own imprisonment. But it was the crucible in which they took the measure of their "deep state" opposition and of the West.

Despite their dramatically improved popular showing in 2002, the Islamists were still clearly a minority faction. Secular Turks harbored profound suspicions. The AKP had been given a chance mainly because the other parties were discredited. The election was not a mandate against secularism but a rebuke of corruption and incompetence. Erdogan is a gifted politician, perceptive enough to know that, while his movement was on the rise, his moment had come prematurely: AKP triumphed more by default than by winning the country over to its supremacist principles. Those principles would have to remain understated, pursued under the radar.

The Islamists would be on a tight leash. They realized that if they failed in their promise to be good stewards of the economy, or if they betrayed their "moderate" bonafides by trying to go too far too fast in the fundamentalist direction, they would surely be turned out in the 2007 elections—if not before.

EXPLOITING THE EU INTEGRATION CHARADE

This "before" possibility was the subject of much pondering. Clearly, the deep state remained the principal obstacle to Islamist ambitions. In the early days, Erdogan was in no position to challenge it head on. He'd have to find ways to erode and nullify it. Still, he had cards to play.

The deep state cared passionately about Europe and America. It had been a Kemalist dream to integrate fully into the West: to be accepted into the European Union (EU); to strengthen ties with the United States—with which the Turks, singularly among Muslim peoples, ingratiated themselves by their membership in NATO as well as their warm trade and military relations with Israel.

Ingeniously, Erdogan grasped the brute, unspoken truth of this dynamic: Turkey would never in a million years be admitted into the EU: Europe's leaders would never tolerate it. But of course, to say this aloud would be so *déclassé*, so downright Islamophobic, that the French and Germans would rather be caught sipping California wine. So rather than be forthright, they have constructed for Turkey an open-ended European integration "process"—and is there anything transnational progressives love more than a "process"? This one is a limitless series of hoops for the Turks to jump through, at the end of which rainbow Ankara will be admitted to the club, probably right around the time hell freezes over or the Euro becomes the world's reserve currency.

Like all Islamists, Erdogan has contempt for Europe and the West. The objective of Muslim supremacists is to dominate and Islamize them, not emulate them. Yet, Erdogan is artfully resourceful enough to exploit to his advantage the Kemalist dream of European integration, and Europe's responsive gamesmanship. For among the

steps Turkey must theoretically climb on the ladder to Euro-worthi-
ness are religious liberty, the separation of religion and the state, and
civilian control of the military.

In their obsession not to be seen as Islamophobic, in their
purblind insistence that aggressive supremacism is not the nature
of mainstream Islam—that, in fact, Islam is the Religion of Peace,
and aggression is *anti*-Islamic—European elites, like their fellow
geniuses in the U.S., assume that they know Islam better than did
such Muslim giants as Ataturk and Banna (to say nothing of iconic
Western thinkers like Churchill and Jefferson, who closely studied
the subject). The blunt fact is that mainstream Middle Eastern Islam
is totalitarianism packaged as "religion," therefore the guidelines
for religions that pose no threat to free societies cannot be applied
to Middle Eastern Islam (the Islam to which Erdogan subscribes)
without putting liberty in grave jeopardy.

In a truly free society, religious liberty is a bedrock. It must
be safeguarded from governmental incursions. If, say, the Chinese
communists cared about such things (they don't), it would make
perfect sense to preclude them from integration with Europe until
they ceased repressing religion (among other things). But an Islamic
society is not free *precisely because of its religion*—or, to put a finer
point on it, because of its dictatorial sharia system, which we inaccurately describe as a mere "religion" due to the spiritual components
that adorn its thoroughgoing regulation of non-spiritual life.

I hasten to add that it is no insult to call sharia a "dictatorial"
and "totalitarian" system. Devout Muslims believe Allah, omnipo-
tent and omniscient, has ordained sharia as the template for virtuous
human life—every detail of that life. In their view, it is profoundly
offensive for his creation, to whom he has deigned to give this gift,
to disobey. One need not be a believer to understand why sharia-
adherent Muslims believe we must all submit. But to understand
this is to appreciate that liberty and sharia cannot share the same
space.

In Turkey, Kemal's government—comprised of Muslims who understood Islam intimately—suppressed Islam not to deny freedom of conscience but to enable it. They were trying to establish exactly the sort of secular civil society Europeans revere, but they knew it could not coexist with sharia. Thus, the government assumed supervision of the country's 80,000 mosques, vetted the imams, controlled the content of sermons and literature, and aggressively monitored Islamic charities. The Muslims running the state understood that Islam would inevitably work against secular civil society if left to its own devices.

The Kemalists' rationale for making the armed forces the secular order's guarantor was not a desire that Turkey be a police state. To the contrary, on the occasions when it has intervened, the Turkish military has hastened to return power to civilian authorities. Indeed, even the *New York Times*—which, flush with Spring Fever, hallucinates elections into democracy, and peremptorily presumes that a military government simply must be more repressive than an elected Islamist government—concedes that the army's 1980 coup was a boon for freer government. The generals were keen to withdraw rapidly from politics and imposed a constitution that, while maintaining the military's guardianship role, enabled the rough-and-tumble of partisan politics and "allowed civilian institutions to bloom."

The Turkish military was given an ultimate constitutional check for the same reason that, whether we choose to acknowledge it or not, Western governments maintain the capacity to impose martial law (albeit, under civilian direction) in dire circumstances. There are times when existential threats to the governing system can only be defeated by military means. The War of 1812 and the American Civil War, during both of which martial law was widely imposed, spring to mind. So does the bloody history of Europe. As Justice Oliver Wendell Holmes Jr. wrote for a unanimous Supreme Court in the 1909 case of *Moyer v. Peabody*, "When it comes to a decision by the head of the State upon a matter involving its life, the ordinary rights of individuals must yield to what he deems the necessities of the moment. Public danger warrants the substitution of executive process for judicial process."

The difference between the governments of Turkey and the United States is that the former is trying to cultivate freedom in an Islamic setting, not preserve freedom in a pre-existing culture of liberty. In a mainstream Islamic society, the threat of reversion to a freedom-devouring sharia societal system always looms. Kemalist Muslims wanted a flourishing civil society but realized they could not keep one unless Islam's supremacist proclivities were permanently checked. Though very far from perfect, they were trying to forge and fortify a prosperous, Western-style nation-state. Contrary to a sharia system, the Kemalists never sought to strangle freedom of conscience. There was never any prohibition on being a Muslim, believing in Islam, or privately adhering to Islam's spiritual elements. It was Islam's *extra-spiritual* aspects (political, social, economic, military, etc.) that were the issue. Without the military as a bulwark against Islamic supremacism, freedom of conscience and liberty in general would be doomed.

This is common sense. It is easily verifiable. Still, Europe will have none of it. It discomfits the conceit that, Islam or no Islam, history marches inexorably toward universal adoption of the Continent's humanist societal model. If the matter were not so serious, it might be tempting to laugh off Europe's hypocrisy: Turkey, of course, is not welcome in the EU precisely because European elites are well aware that Islamic culture *is* different from Western culture. And, as for Europe's end-of-history pretensions, it is far more likely that France and Germany will be conclusively dhimmified than that Turkey will be conclusively Westernized.

All that said, though, the Europeans continue to make believe Turkey will someday be invited to a place at the adults' table if it just addresses a few outdated flaws. Thus Erdogan continues to leverage this European pressure for Turkish reform because it serves the Islamist cause of weakening the Turkish military and, under the ironic guise of "religious liberty," breaking Ataturk's shackles on supremacist Islam.

THE POSTMODERN COUP: A SIGN OF WEAKNESS

Moreover, as the sharply discerning Erdogan realized, the military's 1997 coup actually signaled weakness. Yes, the deep state deep-sixed Erbakan. But the generals were afraid to seize power as they had done in the past. With the West preaching the gospel of irenic Islam, the military apprehended that a full-blown takeover would have unleashed global cataracts of condemnation and lectures about diminished prospects for the holy grail of European integration.

From Erdogan's standpoint, the deep state, for all its huffing and puffing, had not actually tried to stop Erbakan's accession to the premiership when Islamists won the election. Furthermore, even in removing him, the generals demonstrated that they were more cowed by the prospect of Western moralizing than animated to crush a threat to the secular order. Add to that: five short years later, with the post-9/11 West desperate to display that its quarrel was not with Islam but with al Qaeda, the deep state was suddenly content to allow Islamists not just to take control of Parliament, but also to change the law so the reins of power could be handed to a man only recently convicted of sedition. Sizing up matters, Erdogan suspected that Ataturk's constitutional guardians were more paper than tiger. He realized that if he moved gradually and prudently, his seemingly powerful enemies could be ripe for the taking.

Despite his history of rabid Islamic supremacism and anti-Semitism, the West slobbered over Erdogan. As Michael Rubin notes, Colin Powell, the Bush administration's secretary of state, praised Turkey as a "Muslim democracy." This was in keeping with the syncretic sharia constitutions by which the U.S. betrayed democratic culture in Afghanistan and Iraq. It also exasperated authentic Turkish liberals. A dismayed academic quoted by Rubin is typical:

"We are a democracy. Islam has nothing to do with it." Too bad this rudimentary point no longer holds much sway in the West, modern democracy's cradle. Instead, one delusional American diplomat went so far as to paint the AKP as "a Muslim version of a Christian Democratic party."

Such cheerleading paralyzed Turkey's secular democrats, whose concerns, mounting by late 2006, would be waved off by the Bush administration envoy Ross Wilson as "political cacophony." The U.S. and Europe gave Erdogan immense maneuvering room to push Turkey in an Islamist direction. Knowing that the West's ruling class would fawn over his soothing words while averting its eyes from his provocative deeds, Erdogan adopted a winning strategy: publicly disavow any closet agenda to impose sharia law, but work energetically to free Islamic supremacist culture from its Kemalist straitjacket.

CHAPTER EIGHT

The Turkish Model

It is called "the Turkish Model": the Yellow Brick Road to the sparkling Oz of "Islamic Democracy." A roadmap for Egypt, Tunisia, Libya, and the rest; a "template," in the *New York Times*'s telling, "that effectively integrates Islam, democracy and vibrant economics" . . . the "near-impossible dream for Middle East reformers stretching back decades."

It is the crowning achievement of Recep Tayyip Erdogan, *Time Magazine*'s "People's Choice" as the 2011 Person of the Year, and the man the *Times*, the *Economist* and rest of the mainstream press portray as Turkey's "mildly Islamist" prime minister. These, mind you, are the same redoubtable progressives who paint "Tea Party" conservatives and evangelical Christians as wild-eyed extremists, mortal threats to enlightenment and entitlement. But Erdogan— who imposes sharia standards, shunts women out of the workplace, supports jihadists and terror-sponsoring dictators, and capriciously imprisons not only political opponents but, yes, *journalists*—is "mildly Islamic." Go figure.

FAST FRIENDS

Like the left-leaning legacy media, Erdogan himself is a proud proponent of the Turkish Model. These days, when not on one of his frequent roadshows to urge adoption of his template by the "Arab Spring" countries, he is at home hosting his fellow "democrats" from Hamas and the Muslim Brotherhood—or giving his sage counsel to Barack Obama, the U.S. president who publicly cherishes his personal "friendship" with the prime minister.

Indeed, Obama chose Turkey to be the first country he visited as president, the very foundation of his top foreign policy priority: Islamic Outreach. "The bottom line is that we find ourselves in frequent agreement upon a wide range of issues," the president said of Erdogan in March 2012, upon seeking him out at a South Korea summit for advice on the crisis in Syria, the tumult in Egypt, the nukes in Iran—even on the challenges of raising young daughters (both men have two, though the prime minister's are considerably older). The two men's apparent affinity for one another is not difficult to understand; their career arcs merge. Like Erdogan, Obama's roots lie in revolutionary radicalism, sporting among his allies and mentors both terrorists and agitators who spent their adult lives striving to upend the traditional society. Like Obama, Erdogan is making good on his life ambition to fundamentally transform his country.

Nevertheless, in all the gushing over Erdogan by Obama and the Obamedia, an elementary point is lost: The Turkish Model that so enthralls them is inapposite to the Middle East revolts, at least if we are actually talking about *democratization*.

Turkey *already was a democracy* before Erdogan took over. The words of that authentically liberal Turkish academic, so dismayed over the rise of the Islamists, are worth repeating: "We are a democracy. Islam has nothing to do with it." The countries now in the throes of Spring Fever, by contrast, were authoritarian states. The

Arab Spring, if the conventional wisdom is to be believed, is a transition *to* democracy. But the Turkish model is a transition *away from* democracy. Turkey makes sense as a model only if "democracy" is construed not as a culture of liberty and equality but as Erdogan's "train" to Islamization, a train that can travel in either direction.

To be sure, the Turkish Model does have some democratic bunting. The AKP has now been elected three consecutive times, each time by a wider margin, and its plurality is now tantalizingly close to a majority. But this hardly means Turkish Muslims have chosen the light over the darkness. Holding popular elections is no more a decision to live democratically than settling on porcelain plates is a decision about what to eat. Look again at Turkey: the more times Erdogan is elected, and the closer he gets to pushing beyond the 50 percent threshold, the less deference he pays to democratic norms. What the Muslims of Turkey increasingly choose on election day is Islamization, not democracy.

Erdogan wants to impose sharia and fully Islamize Turkish society. For most of his political career, he was brash about this. But he learned from his hard knocks. His heart hasn't changed, but his rhetoric is a bit more inhibited. His strategic aim is still the same, but his tactics walk a razor's edge between constant advance and wary restraint. He must take his supporters ever further down the road, while not getting too far out in front of where they are prepared to go. It takes a deft hand, and he has proved himself extraordinarily able.

SLOW AND STEADY

As a new prime minister, he started with the low-hanging fruit. The AKP moved to criminalize adultery. It loosened the restrictions against both free-lance Koranic instruction and the glorification of Islam in the public schools. It condemned Christianity as a polytheistic religion. It facilitated the banning of alcohol in AKP-controlled municipalities. These initiatives met with broad approval in Islamist quarters and, naturally, they were awkward for non-Islamist Turks to oppose. After all, most of those Turks are Muslims, too; they may not want stricter adherence to classical sharia, but it is difficult for them to oppose—that's why they preferred the Kemalist order, where the government did not permit them to be put to such choices. As they buckled under the new order, Erdogan got a sense of what he could get away with. That license, he knew, would expand over time. For in the bureaucracies—so unnoticed but so critical to how everyday life comes to be lived—Erdogan was stacking the deck with Islamist allies.

In harmony with the ground-up Islamization game-plan of Hassan al-Banna, the Egyptian teacher, Turkish education drew the AKP's laser-like focus. Under Kemalist rule, children were encouraged to proceed through the secular school system and then either learn a trade at vocational school or move on to the Westernized high schools as a prelude to attending university and entering the workplace. Though Islam was tightly monitored and regulated, it was not banned; students who wished to become clerics could tread the alternative path of entry into the "Imam Hatips"—Islamic academies.

Back in 1994, when Mayor/"Imam" Erdogan was proclaiming himself "a servant of sharia" and trying to impose sharia's alcohol ban on Istanbul, he made a promise: "We will turn all our schools into Imam Hatips." As Michael Rubin recounts, upon becoming prime minister, Erdogan moved swiftly to deliver. Under his direction, the law was changed so that Imam Hatip degrees were treated equally with high school degrees. The Islamist thus killed two secular birds with one stone (which certainly has a nice sharia ring): He encouraged greater enrollment in the Islamic academies, prioritizing Islamic over secular education; and he ensured that the universities and, eventually, the professions (very much including government posts) would teem with Islamists who had not assimilated Western fundamentals.

Moreover, Erdogan's AKP moved to establish a glut of new universities. Westerners may have swooned over his apparent determination to enhance Turkey's productivity by broadening its educated base, but that was not the point. Erdogan was reacting to the refusal of the old-line Higher Education Board to bow to his demands that Islamic supremacists be accommodated at the nation's colleges. New universities would enable Erdogan, as Rubin put it, "to handpick rectors and swamp the board with political henchmen." It would promote Islamic indoctrination, and hence the reestablishment of sharia as the social norm.

The AKP also put its stamp on other critical institutions. Erdogan was determined to cultivate an Islamic financial sector. Islamic finance—also known as "Sharia Compliant Finance" (SCF)—is the brainchild of the twentieth-century Muslim intellectual Abul Ala Mawdudi. Besides founding Pakistan's Jamaat-e-Islami party, Mawdudi, who died in 1979, remains a profound influence on both the Muslim Brotherhood and the AKP. The principal purpose of his brainchild, SCF, is economic jihad. As the scholar Daniel Pipes summarizes, SCF aims "to minimize relations with non-Muslims, strengthen the collective sense of Muslim identity, extend Islam into a new area of human activity [i.e., finance], and modernize without Westernizing." In Mawdudi's theory, SCF was inextricably intertwined "with the political, judicial, legal, cultural and social system of Islam." It had to be a core part of any Islamization strategy.

For Erdogan, moreover, promoting SCF was not just a matter of principle. The AKP would come to rely on the Islamic banks to fuel the debt bubble that has masqueraded as sustainable economic prosperity—a key to the party's electoral success. Consequently, upon becoming prime minister, Erdogan purged the Kemalist banking sector, in particular replacing most of the regulatory bureaucracy with Islamic finance specialists.

In addition, as the AKP's growing power opened the prospect of controlling not only the legislature but the office of president—a not trivial but largely ceremonial post under Turkey's current constitution—Erdogan tapped his old chum Abdullah Gul, the SCF expert. Gul was elected in the AKP's 2007 sweep. He is serving a seven-year term, by the conclusion of which Erdogan hopes to have achieved the adoption of a new Constitution, with a powerful presidency . . . that Erdogan would occupy. "Islamic Democracy" begins to sound a lot like Russian "democracy."

The prime minister also moved to lower the mandatory retirement age for various categories of government technocrat. Putting aside the strain this has placed on the budget, it enabled the Islamists to depose incumbents from thousands of positions—including over 40 percent of the republic's 9000 judgeships. In their place, adherents of the AKP's Islamist ideology were installed. Meantime, to degrade further the judiciary's vital role in upholding the secular order, Erdogan refused to enforce judicial rulings and threatened to abolish the Constitutional Court, a key component of the deep state. As the prime minister stepped up Islamization, crushed the rule of law, and paved the way to trump up arrests and prosecutions against his political adversaries and media detractors, U.S. Ambassador Ross Wilson helpfully asserted, "There is nothing that worries me with regards to Turkey's continuation as a strong, secure, stable, secular democracy."

No, nothing at all, I'm sure.

A VEILED THREAT

A single controversy involving the headscarf, a vivid symbol of Islamic piety, speaks volumes about how these and other AKP maneuvers—while refraining from full frontal implementation of sharia—have starkly altered the day-to-day course of Turkish life. As Rubin recounts, Erdogan tellingly skipped the funeral service for a judge who had been murdered in the courthouse by an *Allahu Akbar!*-ranting Islamist lawyer. The jihadist had been protesting the national ban on women's donning of headscarves in both governmental and non-state settings: civil service buildings, courthouses, hospitals, universities, etc.

In small compass, the headscarf *is* the battle between Islamists and secularists. Erdogan knows it, and thus knows the implications of winning it, which he has made an imperative. His repeal campaign turned explosive in 2007 due to two sensational showdowns: Erdogan's wife, Emine, was refused entry into a military hospital upon defiantly declining to remove her headscarf; and a top general refused to shake hands with the wife of President Gul when the First Lady wore a headscarf while accompanying her husband on an official army base tour. The following year, the AKP attempted a statutory repeal, but a 2008 Constitutional Court ruling reinstated the ban.

By then, however, Prime Minister Erdogan had exponentially increased his influence over the bureaucracy. Consequently, the Higher Education Board did not honor the judicial ruling. The law no longer matters, in any event, because it has been overtaken by Erdogan's reshaping of the *culture*. According to the BBC, as many as 60 percent of Turkish women now don the headscarf. Once culture changes, the law conforms to the new reality soon enough. Soner Cagaptay extends this crucial point beyond the veil controversy to the holistic transformation of Turkey under Erdogan's governance. The AKP, he writes:

> introduced new social, political, and foreign policy winds across
> the Turkish society. These forces include solidarity with Islamist
> and anti-Western countries in foreign policy and orthopraxy in
> the public space, promoting outward displays of homogenous
> religious practice and social conservatism, though not necessarily
> directed by faith. After seven years of AKP rule, the Anatolian
> Turks are bending over to the power of the AKP, orthopraxy and
> the Islamist mindset in foreign policy are taking hold. . . [T]he
> number of people identifying themselves as Muslim increased by

ten percent between 2002 and 2007; in addition, almost half of those surveyed describe themselves as Islamist. Moreover, orthopraxy seems to have become internalized: bureaucrats in Ankara now feel compelled to attend prayers lest they be bypassed for promotions. Public display of religious observance, often devoid of faith, has become a necessity for those seeking government appointments or lucrative state contracts.

Is this just democracy in action in a society that honors religious liberty? Concededly, I am a believer in free expression. I'm also predisposed to believe law should reflect culture, not function as the coercive lasso by which our betters drag us to their next panacea. But I have the luxury of living in a (comparatively) free society that grew out of a liberty culture: a nation of nearly 310 million people in which Muslims make up, perhaps, 1 percent of the population—and many, if not most, of those Muslims are moderate, Westernized, believe Islamic law should not be imposed on civil society, and, at least to that extent, are not sharia-adherent as sharia is understood in the Middle East. Tolerance of Muslim sartorial practices and many other benign forms of Islamic orthopraxy are no threat to me or to the vast majority of Americans.

That, however, is not the case in Islamic countries, or in the West's growing number of Islamist enclaves. In such places, the headscarf and its more overtly Islamist derivatives—the veil, hijab, chador, niqab, and burqa—are not simply voluntary expressions of piety. They are submissions to extortion: When some Muslim women shroud themselves in these ways, even freely, pressure to conform intensifies for other Muslim women, and—once an enclave, or a country, is effectively Islamized—for all women, Muslim or not. This is not just the peer pressure that free expression causes in a free society; it is *fear* pressure: coercion and intimidation owing to the well known but little discussed fact that women who fail to cover themselves are often subjected to abuse in Islamic neighborhoods or from their Islamic family members—ranging from cruel taunts to savage violence.

What else has happened in Turkey during the AKP's headscarf jihad? The percentage of women in the workforce has plummeted to only 21 percent (and sliding still), down from 34 percent in 1990—and with a noticeably sharp reduction in the number of women occupying civil service positions. By comparison, the workforce participation rate for women is 59 percent in the United States, 60 percent in the EU, and 54 percent in South Korea.

As David Goldman observes, while Turkey officially places its unemployment rate at 10 percent, it would be over 25 percent if adjusted for the underemployment of Turkish women. In addition, with urbanization shrinking the smallholding agricultural sector, "women who no longer can work the family farm simply sit at home." Increasingly, Islamic mores become more pronounced: it is now less acceptable, and consequently less safe, for Turkish women to be out of the home unless accompanied by their husbands or male family members. Over 12 percent of Turkish women women are illiterate, women thus constituting a stunning 84 percent of the country's estimated five-million illiterate adults.

Meanwhile, as female employment craters, the rate at which women are murdered has zoomed by *1400 percent*. In 2002, when the AKP was first elected, there were sixty-six reported cases of "honor killings"—murders of women and girls at the hands of family members who consider themselves shamed when sharia norms were violated. In just the first seven months of 2009, the number was 953. Domestic violence doubled between 2008 and 2011. A 2009 study cited by Amnesty International concluded that 42 percent of Turkish women between the ages of fifteen and sixty have been victims of domestic violence. Recent court rulings have held that marital rape is not a crime; that repeated sexual assaults on a woman with diminished mental capacity were not rapes because her failure to scream rendered the sex consensual; and that the sentences of twenty-six men convicted of having sex with a thirteen-year-old girl had to be drastically reduced because the girl gave her "consent."

NOT EQUAL, DIFFERENT

These developments should surprise no one. In the Janus-faced style of the Muslim Brotherhood, Erdogan promotes legal sops, like gender-equality laws, but has stated publicly that, as a cultural matter, he does "not believe" in gender equality—adding the Delphic elaboration that he prefers the term "equal opportunity" because "men and women are different in nature, they complete each other." This is the standard Islamic supremacist double-speak when confronted with sharia's discrimination against women: Islamic law does not treat women "worse" than men . . . only "differently from" men. To the contrary, Islamic law proceeds from scriptural assertions, that women, as the prophet Mohammed put it, are "more deficient in intelligence and religion" than men; that "the majority of the dwellers of Hell-fire were [women]; that women may be beaten if they disobey men; and so on.[1] In any event, Erdogan's notion of "equal opportunity" is to tell Turkish women that they should each have at least three children—an argument posited in a "Women's

---

1. See, e.g., Koran Sura 4:34: "Men are the protectors and maintainers of women, because Allah has given the one more (strength) than the other, and because they support them from their means. Therefore the righteous women are devoutly obedient, and guard in (the husband's) absence what Allah would have them guard. As to those women on whose part ye fear disloyalty and ill-conduct, admonish them (first), (next) refuse to share their beds, and last beat them (lightly) . . . "; see also Bukhari, Vol. 1, Book 6, No. 301:

> Once Allah's Apostle went out to the Musalla (to offer the prayer). . . .Then he passed by the women and said, "O women! Give alms, as I have seen that the majority of the dwellers of Hell-fire were you (women)." They asked, "Why is it so, O Allah's Apostle?" He replied, "You curse frequently and are ungrateful to your husbands. I have not seen anyone more deficient in intelligence and religion than you. A cautious sensible man could be led astray by some of you." The women asked, "O Allah's Apostle! What is deficient in our intelligence and religion?" He said, "Is not the evidence of two women equal to the witness of one man?" They replied in the affirmative. He said, "This is the deficiency in her intelligence. Isn't it true that a woman can neither pray nor fast during her menses?" The women replied in the affirmative. He said, "This is the deficiency in her religion."

Day" call for national unity, and in a country where unemployment is already rampant. Moreover, as Anna Louie Sussman reported in the *Atlantic*, the prime minister recently took a gratuitous swipe: removing issues of concern to women from the mission of the relevant government bureaucracy. The "Ministry of Women and Family Affairs" was suddenly renamed the "Ministry of Family and Social Policies." Erdogan could easily, tacitly have modified the agency's mission, but he instead made a point of changing the name.

It was a cipher, communicating the same weltanschauung Erdogan flashed in a television interview when, in describing a woman arrested at a protest, he said he was unsure whether she was a "*kuz*" or a "*kadin*"—i.e., a young virgin or an older, sexually experienced woman. It is an outlook that leaves one unsurprised to learn that, in the World Economic Forum's survey of gender equality, Turkey rates an abysmal 126 out of the 134 countries measured— "lower even than Iran," the *Christian Science Monitor* noted.

Yes, Erdogan claims to seek European integration, but when the European Court of Human Rights upheld the headscarf ban in public schools, he spewed, "It is wrong that those who have no connection to this field make such a decision . . . without consulting Islamic scholars."

That is to say, without applying sharia.

CHAPTER NINE

Joining the Jihad

As his first years in power elucidated, Prime Minister Erdogan had refined his act since the old "Imam of Istanbul" days. It was equally clear, though, that he remained staunchly—not "mildly"—Islamist. "Mildly" Islamist is not going to win the leadership position Erdogan covets in a region that is zealously Islamist.

Remember, an Islamist or (Islamic supremacist) is just a Muslim who favors implementation of Islam's comprehensive social framework cum legal system, sharia. This is why many commentators argue, with great persuasive force, that there is no difference between an "Islamist" and an ordinary Muslim, or between "Islamism" and Islam. As explained in *The Grand Jihad*, I do not subscribe to this approach because there are millions of Muslims who either do not wish to see sharia imposed or who labor to reinterpret sharia so that its acceptance would not require enforcement of its totalitarian, extra-spiritual regulations. We need a term to distinguish those Muslims from the sharia promoters, so it makes sense to denominate the latter as "Islamists." That is not to imply, though, that Islamists are a minority—certainly in the Middle East, they are a strong majority. Nor is it to conclude that the "Islam equals Islamism" commentators do not have a point.

The confusion sown by supremacist Islam's schemers and sympathizers is the conflation of the terms *Islamist* and *terrorist*. But a terrorist is not merely an *Islamist*; he is a *violent jihadist*. Although the concept of *jihad* historically involves the forcible advancement of sharia, it is more accurate these days to call a terrorist a "*violent jihadist*" because, as we have seen, most sharia advancement is accomplished by non-violence. Of course, this stealth jihad, or dawa, would get nowhere were it not for the extortionate climate created by the violent kind. They work hand in hand—the Muslim Brotherhood, for example, leverages both its CAIR agitators and its Hamas terrorists.

Still, the fact that there are violent jihadists committing mass-murder does not make someone devoted to imposing sharia by non-violence a "moderate." *Pace* the legacy media, being "moderate" in comparison to, say, Osama bin Laden, does not make Muslim leaders in the Erdogan mold "mildly Islamist"—especially in light of Erdogan's own strident rejection of modifiers like "moderate" as insulting to Muslims. Indeed, by his own logic, Erdogan would be offended even by the gentle term "Islamist"—to say nothing of the more cuddly "mildly Islamist." Erdogan believes that Islam is sharia-adherent *by definition*, placing him, on this question, in the same theoretical pew as not only the "Islam equals Islamism" proponents but also al Qaeda and the Muslim Brotherhood. Therefore, he denies the distinguishing gloss urged by those of us who hope Islamic reformers can succeed. No moderation for him: "Islam is Islam, and that's it." And if we're talking strictly about the Middle East, Erdogan is right.

A CHILL BREEZE BLOWS THROUGH EVERY ARAB SPRING

While the prime minister might no longer be the aspiring writer/ director/star of *Maskomya* fame, he has also remained a dyed-in-the-wool anti-Zionist and anti-Semite. Americans—at least those not named Bush or Obama—might have thought this a tad problematic. After all, in the years preceding Erdogan's accession, Turkey, our NATO partner, had enjoyed warm relations with Israel, our closest ally in the region. Their intercourse extended to sensitive military matters: intelligence-sharing, joint training, and a robust trade in sophisticated weaponry. Turkey and Israel also cooperated closely on regional concerns, especially the emerging nuclear threat posed by the Shiite Islamist regime in Iran, and the various provocations of Bashar al-Assad's barbarous dictatorship in Syria—Iran's client state and fellow co-sponsor of Hamas and Hezbollah. Like Israel, moreover, Turkey's government was closely allied not only with the United States but also with NATO countries in Europe—on which Turkey, even more than Israel, is economically dependent. For Turkey, then, bonds with Israel were of deep political, financial, cultural, and national-security significance.

Alas, the attraction the Jewish state holds for the Kemalist deep state has never been shared by the population at large. Anti-Semitism and anti-Zionism run rampant in Turkey, just as they do throughout the Arab Middle East (and in the metastasizing Muslim enclaves of Europe). In the hands of the right demagogue, Jew hatred, like anti-Americanism, can serve as the glue that unites disparate Muslim factions.

Erdogan's mentor, Necmettin Erbakan, made anti-Semitic incitement a core part of his program. Such appeals resonate in a Muslim culture because they can be firmly rooted in Islamic doctrine. The leitmotif of hostility to Jews is patent in Islamic scripture and culture—e.g., accusations that they are responsible for killing Allah's prophets and that Allah will take his vengeance against them at the end of time.[1] The Muslim Brotherhood makes copious resort to this oeuvre. For instance, the originating 1988 charter of its Palestinian faction,

---

1. See also Andrew G. Bostom, *The Legacy of Islamic Antisemitism: From Sacred Texts to Solemn History* (Prometheus Books 2008); Bat Ye'or, *Europe Globalization, and the Coming of the Universal Caliphate* (Fairleigh Dickinson University Press 2011).

Hamas, expressly frames the destruction of Israel as a sacred Islamic duty. It further quotes an end-of-days hadith (Sahih Muslim Book 41, No. 6985), which is well known to those who do not limit their news diet to the legacy media menu. In it, the prophet Mohammed promises that Allah will help the Muslims exterminate all remaining Jews:

> The Prophet, Allah bless him and grant him salvation, has said: "The Day of Judgment will not come about until Muslims fight the Jews [killing the Jews], when the Jew will hide behind stones and trees. The stones and trees will say, 'Oh Muslims, oh Abdulla, there is a Jew behind me, come and kill him.' "

A longtime confederate of the Brotherhood, Erbakan seamlessly adopted this emphasis on sacralized animus against Judaism. So did his protégés, including Erdogan.

Jew hatred is that lowest of common denominators, the chill breeze blowing through every Arab Spring. As the Middle East Media Research Institute reported in 2005 (i.e., three years into Erdogan's first term), anti-Zionism and anti-Semitism are staples of the Turkish press, just as they are in the Arab media. The point of the spear is Istanbul's daily, *Milli Gazete*, house organ of the Erbakan/Erdogan faction since the early Seventies. It regularly portrays Jews as "characteristic[ally] . . . savage [and] treacherous." Typical is this:

> "Judaism" is synonymous with "treason" . . . . They even betrayed God. . . . When God told them to bow their heads while entering Al-Quds [Jerusalem], they entered with their heads up. The prophets sent to them, such as Zachariah and Isaiah, were murdered by the Jews. . . . In fact, no amount of pages or lines would be sufficient to explain the Koranic chapters and our Lord Prophet's [i.e., Mohammed's] words that tell us of the betrayals of the Jews.

Welcome to "mildly Islamist" rhetoric.

It is simply a fact that such rants find a receptive audience in Turkey, just as they do in all the region's Muslim lands—very much including the new, "Made in the U.S.A." Iraq, the "Islamic democracy" that collaborates with Iran but still has no diplomatic relations with Israel. Prime Minister Erdogan exploits this anti-Semitic zeitgeist. He does so philosophically because he is an Islamic supremacist, wedded to the fiction that Israel, the ancestral Jewish homeland for centuries before Mohammed's birth, is an illegitimate occupation of Islamic land. He does so tactically because bashing Israel and Jews drives a wedge between Turkey and the West, and between millions of Turkish Muslims and the Kemalist deep state that has been so cozy with the ummah's all-purpose villains.

EMBRACING TERROR

Hamas and Hezbollah are terrorist organizations and regarded as such under U.S. law. Hezbollah is responsible for killing hundreds of Americans in addition to Israelis; Hamas operatives, who have also murdered Americans, are often prosecuted in the United States for providing material support to terrorism. Yet Erdogan has made a point of embracing both jihadist groups on the world stage. Plainly, his status as prime minister of a NATO ally is a trifle when it conflicts with the imperative of Islamist solidarity.

Case-in-point: Yasin al-Qadi, a shady Saudi financier formally designated as an international terrorist, under both U.S. law and U.N. Security Council resolutions. Qadi ran a Muslim charitable front, the Muwafaq Foundation, which, according to the U.S. Treasury Department, "transferred millions to [Osama] bin Laden"; provided "logistical and financial support for a >*mujahideen* battalion in Bosnia"; and provided the camouflage of ostensibly legitimate employment to terrorists at its offices in Sudan, Somalia, and Pakistan. Furthermore, an FBI affidavit directly implicated Qadi in the funnelling of $820,000 to Hamas, and the feds additionally tied him to funding for the deadly Abu Sayyaf jihadist organization in the Philippines.[2] On the basis of this evidence from American law-enforcement and intelligence services, the U.N. resolutions obliged member nations to freeze Qadi's assets.

Yet Erdogan publicly vouched for the terrorist. In 2006, the Turkish press reported that Erdogan's confidant and AKP co-founder, H. Cuneyd Zapsu, had donated money to Qadi, in addition to being in business with him. When questions were raised, the prime minister bristled: "I know Mr. Qadi. I believe in him as I believe in myself. For Mr. Qadi to associate with a terrorist organization, to support one, is impossible." Though Turkey had frozen Qadi's assets and commenced an investigation of his companies in 2001 (i.e., before the AKP came to power), Erdogan refused to enforce the freeze. "I trust him," the prime minister said, "the same way I trust my father."

Forbes uncovered evidence strongly suggesting that Qadi, whose knot of Islamist friends includes several politicians and businessmen in Erdogan's orb, was able to access funds in Turkey through complex transactions executed after Erdogan's accession. Later in 2006, a top prosecutor in Istanbul suddenly dropped Turkey's case against Qadi, proclaiming, "Al-Qadi is a philanthropic businessman and no connection has been found between him and terrorist organizations." The Finance Ministry's chief investigator complained that, once the AKP took over, the lead agents on his probe of Qadi were reassigned and his investigation was undermined by government bureaucrats in what bordered on "obstruction of justice."

Erdogan's position is not difficult to decipher . . . if we allow ourselves to think through the ramifications of *Islamizing* a country, rather than *democratizing* it. In Islamist theory, Hamas, to take a prominent example, is not a *terrorist* organization. As we've seen,

---

2.   Andrew C. McCarthy, "Can Libel Tourism Be Stopped?" (*Commentary*, Sept. 2008) (http://www.commentarymagazine.com/viewarticle.cfm/can-libel-tourism-be-stopped–12502) (subscription required).

"terrorism" is what happens when *Muslims* are killed, particularly by non-Muslims. To Islamic supremacists, Hamas is a *resistance* force, fighting in a laudable jihad to drive infidel occupiers out of what is deemed Muslim territory. Al Qaeda also gets a pass on this "resistance" rationale, at least when it narrows its terror targets to non-Muslims operating in Islamic lands. That is why Erdogan's Muslim Brotherhood soul-mates considered Osama bin Laden a *"mujahid"*—a term of honor for a jihad warrior.[3]

Erdogan knows exactly what he's doing. When he says his friend Qadi has nothing to do with "terrorism," he knows that Westerners take this to mean "Qadi must not have committed the alleged offenses." He also knows that the audience he most cares about, the ummah, understands him to be saying something quite different: "Sure, Qadi may have done these things, but they do not constitute terrorism." This is a dissimulation tactic that Islamists have perfected, largely because their Western pom-pom wavers would rather be lied to than face the dire implications of the truth.

TARGETING ISRAEL

Although Erdogan had to wait until he was in a stronger position to challenge the deep state, he had no such reticence when it came to championing Muslim terrorists at Israel's expense. He knew this would be broadly popular in Turkey. As his support base grew, he could more confidently set about cutting his opposition down to size.

In spring 2004, only a year into his premiership, Erdogan bitterly condemned Israel for the targeted killings of Hamas's founders, Sheikh Ahmad Yassin and Abdel Aziz Rantisi. Hamas and its allies

---

3.   As I recounted in *The Grand Jihad*, at pp. 68-69, *mujahid* was the honorific applied to bin Laden in 2008 by Muhammad Mahdi Akef, then the Brotherhood's Supreme Guide. Akef rejected the suggestion that bin Laden was a "terrorist," exclaiming, "I support his activities against the occupiers." He added that, in his "sincerity in resisting the occupation," bin Laden was "close to Allah on high."

consider themselves in a state of constant war against Israel and were, at the time, executing numerous suicide bombings—in just the five-week span before Israeli forces retaliated, jihadists killed thirty-three Israelis and wounded 156 in four major attacks. When the IDF inevitably struck back, it carefully homed in on the two Hamas leaders, abjuring the Palestinian-style mass murder of civilians. Yet, Erdogan reacted to the deaths of Yassin and Rantisi by accusing Israel of "state terrorism." The outburst stunned Israel, whose diplomats protested angrily.

Israel and the West would have to get used to being stunned by Erdogan's affection for the Muslim Brotherhood's Palestinian terrorist branch. Weeks later, Erdogan went out of his way to exacerbate the tension. With Israel's deputy prime minister in Ankara, Turkey's prime minister declined to see him, claiming to be too busy. Yet he managed to find time that same day to meet with Muhammad Naji al-Otari, the prime minister of *Syria*. It was a snub with teeth, informing Israel and the West that they were now dealing with an "Islamic democracy," not the democracy they'd previously known.

It is an "Islamic democracy" that has its own ideas about "outreach." After Hamas won the Palestinian election in January 2006, Erdogan acted swiftly to confer sovereign legitimacy on the jihadists and to undermine Bush administration efforts to continue marginalizing them (efforts President Bush and his State Department had themselves undermined by supporting the election—as "democracy" promotion—in the first place). Though American and European leaders insisted that Hamas would be isolated until they renounced terrorism and accepted Israel's right to exist, Erdogan hosted Hamas's leadership in Ankara less than a month after the election. Moreover, he continued to champion the terrorists even after, a few months later, Hamas switched from the democracy "train" to the coup express, brutally ousting Palestinian Authority forces from Gaza.

Erdogan's reasoning in siding with Hamas over Fatah is easily gleaned. Hamas was created because the Muslim Brotherhood found

Yasser Arafat's leadership of the Palestine Liberation Organization too light on Islamic supremacism and too redolent of the Nasserite turn to secular Leftism. Previously, Islamists ardently supported the PLO because, if you wanted to destroy Israel, the PLO was the only game in town. With the 1987 emergence of Hamas, however, there arose an Islamic supremacist alternative that not only portrayed Israel's elimination by violent jihad as an Islamic obligation but, furthermore, explicitly tied this effort into the Muslim Brotherhood's global Islamization program. Erdogan knows what team he is on.

The following year, Erdogan demonstrated that his democracy "train" likes to spread the wealth around to the wide variety of Israel's terrorist tormentors—in much the same manner as Iran. Fittingly, we learn this from a derailment. As Michael Rubin notes, Turkish emergency personnel responding when a train went off the tracks in 2007 found it to be ferrying a cache of weapons for delivery to Hezbollah in Lebanon.

As Erdogan abetted the terrorists, the terrorists continued their war against Israel. Hamas, in particular, exploited its control over Gaza to step up the pace of rocket attacks against Israeli civilian centers. In 2008 alone, 1,750 rockets and 1,528 mortar shells were fired into Israel. Hamas's arsenal is comparatively crude and its competence is middling, so its attacks terrorize Israelis but tend not to kill very many. Still, a barrage of this kind cannot be ignored forever. Thus in late 2008, the Israelis responded with Operation Cast Lead, four weeks of air-strikes against Hamas installations (which the terrorist organization typically embeds in civilian infrastructure to make retaliatory attacks politically problematic). The aerial attacks were complemented, in the final stages, by ground troops, which conducted combat missions against Hamas forces. The IDF is famously competent. Its responsive raids were withering, killing 1,300 Palestinians, injuring thousands more, and causing massive property damage—compared with just ten Israeli soldiers and thee Israeli civilians killed.

OBAMA ENTERS AND ERGODAN DOUBLES DOWN

There was a time when going to war meant defeating the enemy by breaking his will. If a sovereign state were provoked by thousands of rocket and mortar attacks from an enemy that proudly brays its intention to destroy that sovereign state, it was to be expected that there would be retaliation massive enough to force a surrender and ceasefire on favorable terms. That was before the media started getting its talking points from transnational progressive legions of "international humanitarian law" activists, who seem to have only slightly less antipathy for Israel than do the Palestinians. The Left has thus skewed the military doctrine of "proportionality."

Classically, proportionality, and its companion concept, "distinction," called for field commanders to weigh the military advantage to be derived from a combat operation against the risk of *inordinate* collateral damage to civilian lives and infrastructure—mindful of the fact that the objective of war is victory and that some civilian casualties are inevitable, even when the enemy is not comprised of terrorist operatives secreting themselves among civilian supporters. In the calculus of international humanitarian law advocates, however, war is always worse than whatever provoked it, victory is not a permissible goal, and proportionality is a puerile comparison of one side's casualties versus the other. At least that is how it works when many more Palestinians than Israelis are killed; as we've seen, when Palestinians kill dozens of Israeli civilians and Israel responds by killing exactly two Hamas leaders, proportionality goes unmentioned and Israel is slandered for practicing "state terrorism." This convenient arrangement is an Allah-send for terrorists, who get to provoke the fight and then paint any response as a "violation of international law."

Thus was born the global Islamist propaganda campaign to smear Israel as a war criminal disproportionately slaying innocent Palestinian civilians. Leading the parade was . . . Erdogan, doubtless emboldened by Barack Obama's late 2008 triumph in the U.S.

presidential election. The new administration's signals were unmistakable: Obama was anxious to address Islamic grievances (real or imagined) and retreat from America's former posture as a reliable supporter of Israel's national defense concerns (existentially real).

As Americans marked President Obama's inauguration, Erdogan stepped up his inflammatory rhetoric, accusing Israel of committing "a serious crime against humanity," and inveighing that "killing innocent people, defenseless children and women, bombing civilians, and using disproportionate force are unacceptable."[4] The Jewish state, he acidly sniped, had turned Gaza into a "concentration camp." Meanwhile, Erdogan contrived a public dressing-down of Israeli President Shimon Peres at the annual World Economic Forum in Davos. Peres, an icon of the Israeli Left, passionately defended Israel's response to Hamas's war of jihadist aggression. Pouncing, Erdogan railed, "President Peres, you are old, and your voice is loud out of a guilty conscience. When it comes to killing, you know very well how to kill. I know well how you hit and kill children on beaches." He then stormed off the stage—a fitting finish since "staged" perfectly describes the performance.

The day before the Davos panel, AKP partisans were given the heads-up to prepare for a rally in the wee hours of the morn. Istanbul's subway engineers were instructed to keep the trains running long after the usual midnight shutdown. When the plane arranged after Erdogan's "unexpectedly" early departure from Switzerland touched down at 3 a.m. in Turkey, the prime minister was "spontaneously" greeted by a throng of 3,000 supporters, waving Palestinian flags and signs hailing Erdogan as an Islamist hero. As Michael Rubin tartly observed, "Even in a city as vibrant as Istanbul, it is hard to purchase Palestinian flags by the thousand after the close of business."

By late March, 2009, a new low was achieved in American-Israeli relations. As the Obama administration pressured Israel to

---

4.   Merley, *Turkey, the Global Muslim Brotherhood, and the Gaza Flotilla* p. 35.

97

cease construction of settlements in East Jerusalem, the president invited Prime Minister Benjamin Netanyahu to the White House for negotiations. When Netanyahu refused to back down, Obama, in a breathtaking snub, bolted in a huff and went off to dinner with his family, leaving the Israeli prime minister stranded in a White House meeting room. Simultaneously, the Obama-Erdogan romance was heating up. The administration announced that Obama had chosen Turkey as the first country he would visit as president. There, in early April, he was warmly embraced by Erdogan and took pains to renounce the notion that America was "at war with Islam"—an Islamist narrative that Obama dignified by repeating.

For Erdogan, the message was clear: there would be no American push-back against his open and notorious support of the Islamist onslaught against Israel. The AKP government scaled back all intelligence and military cooperation with Israel, dismantling a strategic partnership that had been in place for two decades. IDF planes were barred from using Turkish air space for training purposes. Erdogan froze arms trading and maintenance agreements between the two countries. Turkey even refused to participate in joint naval exercises with the United States because Israel had been invited to take part. With no meaningful U.S. resistance, the prime minister was making manifest that Turkey was now an Islamic supremacist power, fully onboard with the overarching jihadist goal of strangling the Jewish state.

CHAPTER TEN

Champion of Hamas

Visions of "Islamic democracy" induce Spring Fever in the West. In the Middle East, though, spring is when a young Muslim's fancy turns to thoughts of destroying Israel. Come to think of it, in summer, autumn and winter, too—and not just the young.

Even at eighty-six years of age, and having only recently tied the knot for a third time (in June 2012, with a Moroccan woman nearly forty years his junior), Sheikh Yusuf al-Qaradawi remains obsessed. As the Brotherhood eminence related in 2009, to a crowd of his disciples and to millions more watching on al-Jezeera, "The only thing I hope for is that, as my life approaches its end, Allah will give me an opportunity to go to the land of jihad and resistance, even if in a wheelchair. I will shoot Allah's enemies, the Jews, and they will throw a bomb at me, and thus, I will seal my life with martyrdom."

For the time being, though, Qaradawi contents himself with raising money "to support Palestinians fighting occupation," for "if we can't carry out acts of jihad ourselves, we should at least support and prop up the mujahideen financially and morally so that they will be steadfast until God's victory."[11] With the rise of Prime Minister Erdogan, with whom Qaradawi is an oft-time interlocutor, Turkey has become fertile ground indeed for the sustenance of Hamas.

THE AKP AND THE BROTHERHOOD

After the establishment of AKP rule, Turkey became the jihadist hub of Ataturk's nightmares. Hamas and its patrons in the global Muslim Brotherhood began holding many of their confabs in Istanbul. The "Muslims of Europe Conference" in July 2006, for example, drew not only Qaradawi but such notables as the Brotherhood's Tunisian emir Rashid Ghannouchi; the Swiss academic Tariq Ramadan (grandson on Hassan al-Banna himself, and son of Sa'id Ramadan, who forged the Brotherhood's now substantial presence in Europe); and both Ibrahim el-Zayat and Fouad Alaoui, the Brotherhood's chiefs in, respectively, Germany and France. Also in attendance were several of Turkey's own leading governmental Islamists, including Mehmet Aydin, Erdogan's Chairman of Religious Affairs. Soon, two other Qaradawi-controlled entities, the European Council on Fatwa and Research and the International Union of Muslim Scholars, also began holding conferences in Istanbul. High-ranking AKP figures reliably attended, bathing in the glow of scholarly celebration: Turkey lauded as the former and "potential future nexus of the Islamic world."[2]

Another important Qaradawi enterprise is the Union for Good (sometimes translated as the "Union of Good"), a coalition of Islamic "charities" established after the outbreak of the second Palestinian Intifada against Israel in late 2000. Its primary purpose is to raise money for Hamas. Sharia is the reason for placing scare-quotes around the word *charities*.

---

1. Levitt, *Hamas*, pp. 63-64.
2. Merley, *Turkey, the Global Muslim Brotherhood, and the Gaza Flotilla*, pp. 44-47.

As we saw in Chapter 3, the Islamic obligation of *zakat*, though benignly rendered as "charitable giving" by the Western media—taking its talking points from the Muslim Brotherhood, just like Western politicians do—actually involves sustaining the ummah, exclusive of non-Muslims. More to the point, sharia—i.e., the classical version of sharia endorsed by al-Azhar scholars and the Muslim Brotherhood think-tank, the International Institute of Islamic Thought—explicitly calls for an eighth of the donation haul to be dedicated to jihadists waging war against non-Muslims. When you read innumerable reports that charitable funds have been "diverted" to terrorist ends, you are reading pure tripe. Sharia is very clear that supporting jihad is, in part, the *precise intent* of zakat . . . and Qaradawi projects are nothing if not sharia compliant. No surprise, then, that the Union for Good has long been formally designated as a foreign terrorist organization under American law. To provide it with funding or other assistance is deemed material support to terrorism, a serious crime.

Nevertheless, a Turkish "charity" known as the Humanitarian Relief Foundation or IHH (*İnsan Hak ve Hürriyetleri ve İnsani Yardım Vakfı*) is a member organization of Qaradawi's Union for Good. In truth, IHH is a jihadist organization camouflaged as a global do-gooder, recognized by the UN as one of hundreds of "humanitarian" Non-Governmental Organizations (NGOs). Founded in the early Nineties by Osman Atalay, a Turkish Islamist who fought in the jihad in Bosnia, the outfit has longstanding ties to Muslim Brotherhood satellites across the world. Its connections to Turkey's Islamic supremacist political parties, particularly the Refah party and, later, the AKP, are so intimate that the Turkish press has referred to IHH, tongue firmly in cheek, as a "GNGO"—as in, *Governmental* Non-Governmental Organization. It claims to have an annual budget of about $100 million. Whatever the true amount is, the IHH priority is Islamization, not charity. And it doesn't just work the financial end; as we shall see, IHH operatives also dabble in the jihad's grislier aspects.

In a rare exhibition of bipartisan clarity, the United States Senate voted overwhelmingly in June 2010 to recommend that the Obama administration investigate IHH in anticipation of formally designating it as a terrorist organization. No wonder: IHH has received funding from the Success Foundation, an organization headed by the now-convicted terrorist financier Abdurahman Alamoudi (whom we met in Chapter 3). It has also gotten donations from the International Islamic Relief Organization, a Saudi "charity" whose leaders have included Osama bin Laden's brother-in-law, Mohammad Jamal Khalifa, and two of whose branches are formally designated as foreign terrorist organizations under American law. IHH uses some of the money it raises to subsidize the families of Hamas suicide bombers.

Moreover, as the *Wall Street Journal* has reported, a French terrorism investigation in the 1990s determined that IHH has provided logistical support (such as phony travel documents, safe haven, and possibly firearms) to terrorists. Jean-Louis Bruguiere, the French investigative magistrate who handled the case, contends that the IHH was complicit in the jihadist "Millennium plot" to bomb Los Angeles International Airport in late 1999, and was "basically helping al Qaeda when bin Laden started to want to target U.S. soil." A French intelligence report further asserts that IHH phone records show repeated calls in 1996 to an al Qaeda guesthouse in Milan. The Obama State Department will not confirm IHH's al Qaeda ties, but it has acknowledged that IHH officials have consulted with senior Hamas figures at rendezvous in Turkey, Syria, and Gaza over the last several years. In May 2011, IHH added its voice to other Islamist groups in Turkey's "Islamic democracy" by denouncing the U.S. military's killing of Osama bin Laden, labeling it "American terrorism."

Despite this record, or, more accurately, because of it, the IHH membership list reads like a *Who's Who in Erdogan's AKP*. IHH's former chairman, Eyup Fatsa, is an AKP member of Parliament, and is believed by Israeli intelligence to have forged the alliance between IHH and AKP in the late Nineties. According to the *New York Times*, the IHH-AKP roster also includes IHH founder Zeyid Aslan, a member of the Turkish Parliament who heads the Turkey-Palestine Interparliamentary Friendship Group; Ahmet Faruk Unsal, who served five years in Parliament after being elected in the AKP victory of 2002; Mehmet Emin Sen, the former AKP mayor of a township in Anatolia; Murat Mercan, a senior party official and chairman of the Turkish Parliament's foreign affairs committee; and Ali Yandir, the AKP official who runs the Istanbul City Municipality Transportation Corporation—a bureaucratic connection of considerable significance, we shall see.

IHH often coordinates with Prime Minister Erdogan's office and campaigns vigorously for him, shoring up critical support from Turkish Islamists, particularly in the merchant class. In addition, the organization has received awards for excellence from AKP government officials, including Bulent Arinc, formerly the Speaker of Parliament and now Erdogan's deputy prime minister. As nicely captured by Turkey's widely read daily, *Hurriyet News*, "There can be no mistake that the Erdogan government is morally and politically behind this group."

BREAKING THE BLOCKADE

After Hamas's 2008 rocket siege prompted Israel's responsive Operation Cast Lead, which Erdogan lambasted as a "crime against humanity," Sheikh Qaradawi exhorted Muslims the world over to observe a "Day of Anger." IHH mobilized to assist Hamas. Zeyid Aslan, the aforementioned IHH trustee and leading AKP parliamentarian, accused Israel of "genocide" against the Palestinians. IHH leader Bulen Yildirim, who enjoys warm relations with Erdogan, met with Hamas's top political official, Khaled Mashaal, in Syria before attending a Hamas rally in Gaza. There, Yildirim proclaimed, "All of those who do not stand by the Palestinian people will meet their end and destruction," and that "all the Islamic people will demand that their leaders become like Recep Tayyip Erdogan."[3]

In May 2009, IHH cosponsored a "World Popular Conference for the Support of Palestine" in Istanbul. Featured were Qaradawi, Yildirim, AKP officials Aslan and Cemal Yilmaz Demir, representatives from the violent jihadist groups Hamas, Hezbollah, and Palestinian Islamic Jihad, and an array of global Muslim Brotherhood grandees, including Ghannouchi of Tunisia, Jamal Badawi, a pioneer of the Brotherhood's American network, and Mohammed Akram Adlouni—secretary-general of the al-Quds [Jerusalem] International Institutionand author of the "Explanatory Memorandum" outlining the Brotherhood's "grand jihad" to destroy the West. Steven Merley of the Jerusalem Center for Public Affairs provides the flavor of the rally. Sheikh Qaradawi insisted that to help the Palestinian "resistance" is "not a contribution—it is an obligation" to be satisfied by "financial means." Adlouni, meanwhile, lionized Erdogan for tearing into Israel's president at Davos, reaffirming that "Turkey is still the caliphate as the center of our lives in our heart. I wish all the Arab countries would follow Turkey's example by taking this stance. Israel is trying to Judaize Jerusalem!"[4]

By late 2009, IHH joined a coalition of Islamist and Leftist organizations, led by Viva Palestina and the Free Gaza Movement, in a confederation to break what they describe as Israel's "siege of Gaza." Front and center of the scheme was George Galloway, a radical Leftist and notorious Hamas supporter who was reelected to the British Parliament in 2012. The coalition's modus operandi was (and, as this is written, remains) to organize ostensible "humanitarian aid" caravans, for the true purpose of challenging the restrictions around Gaza's borders.

---

3. Merley, *Turkey, the Global Muslim Brotherhood, and the Gaza Flotilla*, pp. 61-64.

4. Merley, *Turkey, the Global Muslim Brotherhood, and the Gaza Flotilla* p. 70.

It is worth remembering why these restrictions—tightly guarded land crossings, closely patrolled air space, and a sea blockade—were put in place. In 2005, Israel unilaterally withdrew from the Gaza Strip, territory it had captured from Egypt during wars of Arab-Muslim aggression designed to destroy the Jewish state. The withdrawal, which involved the painful dismantling of settlements and forced evacuation of Israeli citizens, was an olive branch extended to Palestinians and their jihadist leaders. Common sense, of course, says that appeasing terrorists results only in more terrorism. More terrorism is precisely what Israel got.

Hamas characteristically took the concession as weakness rather than civility. The violent jihad, involving thousands of rocket attacks, only intensified. Israel abided even this campaign while under intense international pressure to pretend that Hamas's rival Palestinian faction, the marginally less rabid Fatah, was a worthy negotiating partner. But when Hamas followed up its "democratic" electoral victory in early 2006 by forcibly ousting Fatah from Gaza in the June 2007 coup, Israel had no choice but to seal the parts of Gaza's borders that it controls. Egypt, too, shares a border with Gaza, but the Mubarak regime in Egypt simultaneously sealed it due to what the U.S. Congressional Research Service described, with unwitting prescience, as "concern for the possibly destabilizing effects of Hamas's relations with the Egyptian Muslim Brotherhood, which the government of President Mubarak considers a threat."

The vital purposes of the blockade are obvious—at least to anyone who is neither an Islamic supremacist nor a transnational progressive living safely in the West: namely, protect Israeli citizens from suicide terrorism, prevent arms shipments from reaching the jihadists, and pressure the Palestinians into real negotiations. Alas, the latter would call for acceptance of two conditions that Hamas, in its incorrigible anti-Semitism and anti-Zionism, is too barbaric to contemplate: conceding Israel's right to exist and renouncing terrorism (meaning, *truly* renounce it, without the deceptive caveat that "resistance" is ... um, kosher).

Even the U.N., though notoriously quick to condemn Israeli defense measures, acknowledged the blockade's propriety in a lengthy 2011 special report. By contrast, the portrayal of the blockade by Erdogan & Co. as a humanitarian catastrophe—one that purportedly renders Gaza a "concentration camp"—takes propaganda to the level of obscenity.

Israel liberally permits the importation of food, medicine, other necessities, and many luxury items. What it bars are munitions and "dual-use" items that would materially support Hamas and the jihadist campaign by which Palestinians choose to be the enemies of their own prosperity. There is no humanitarian reason to challenge the blockade because Israel liberally allows humanitarian deliveries after they undergo an inspection. Yet, echoing Qaradawi, Galloway bellowed that, in the wake of Operation Cast Lead, "actions speak louder than words" and that the best anti-Israel strategy was "to try to create a siege."

This is exactly what the Leftist-Islamist coalition did, to disastrous effect, in January 2010. A convoy launching from London in early December 2009, carrying eighty vehicles loaded with what was described as "medical, humanitarian and educational aid," was enthusiastically greeted in Istanbul less than two weeks later. Top Erdogan government officials, including the deputy prime minister, foreign minister, and the speaker of parliament, feted a convoy delegation that included Galloway, IHH President Yildirim, and the aforementioned Aslan (honcho of both the IHH and AKP). Thereafter, IHH merged another sixty-two vehicles into the convoy, packed with similar cargo. The full caravan set out on the drive to Gaza, by way of Syria, Jordan, and finally Egypt. Along for the ride were over 200 Turkish citizens (about half the total in the convoy), including several senior AKP members. Prominent among the latter was Murat Marjan, chairman of the Turkish Parliament's foreign affairs committee.

In Egypt, the convoy endeavored to enter Gaza through the Rafah Crossing. The Mubarak government, however, refused to allow the entire convoy to cross into the Strip, insisting that some of the vehicles would have to try entering through Israel. An angry confrontation resulted, with agitators rebuking Egyptian riot troops as pawns of the Zionist enemy. Demonstrators began pelting the troops with stones, prompting them to open fire. In the ensuing melee, a Palestinian gunman shot an Egyptian soldier to death, while two Palestinian demonstrators were wounded and dozens of other people were injured.

The Egyptian government relented and allowed all convoy participants to enter Gaza briefly—to deliver their wares and leave immediately—only after top officials in Erdogan's government, including Foreign Minister Ahmet Davutoglu, interceded with their counterparts in Cairo. Once in Gaza, the AKP government officials in tow were warmly embraced by Ismail Haniyeh, Hamas's Gaza chief. Haniyeh is formally recognized by Erdogan's government as the "Palestinian Prime Minister," which is what taking the Islamic "democracy train" to the jihadist coup station will get you. Alluding to the AKP emir's upbraiding of Shimon Peres at Davos, Haniyeh yipped, "We still haven't forgotten Prime Minister Erdogan's courageous act in the face of Israel's attacks and blockade." "With the new policy Turkey has been pursuing," he added, "the Middle East is also being reshaped."

Indeed.

THE *MAVI MARMARA*

In late January 2010, shortly after the triumphant return of AKP legislators and IHH activists from Haniyeh's lair, the IHH announced plans for yet another joint caravan with the Free Gaza Movement.

This time, the venture would be a springtime "Freedom Flotilla" of several boats that would challenge what IHH described as Israel's "illegal blockade" of Gaza—"a mockery of international law." (IHH's apparently abridged version of that corpus omits the part about self-defense, the natural sovereign right that is the venerable foundation of international law.)

Yildirim, the IHH president and a prominent figure known to have close AKP connections, foreshadowed the violence to come. Passengers, he asserted, would defend themselves if Israeli forces confronted the flotilla. He vowed to "break the siege," further declaring that "[i]f al-Quds [Jerusalem] will be in Muslim hands, the whole world will be in Muslim hands. . . .;The present rulers of Jerusalem are the Jews, the Zionists. All the suffering and the evil in the world today is a result of that. Therefore Jerusalem must be liberated." Yildirim futher predicted that Israel would not dare interfere with the flotilla because attacking one of the ships would be "the same as attacking a Turkish consulate." Still, palpably spoiling for a fight, he later sniped, "We are sailing to Gaza as human shields."[5]

The purported "Freedom Flotilla" was, in fact, ardently supported by Erdogan's government. Put aside for a moment the fact that several regime officials were active participants in the prior convoy that provoked murderous rioting in Egypt. On May 12, 2010, Erdogan met in Istanbul with representatives of the European Campaign to End the Siege of Gaza—a Muslim Brotherhood-dominated outfit that had its own ship in the flotilla. After the meeting, members of the group reported Erdogan's vow that Turkey intended to end Israel's blockade.[6] Three days later, on May 15, Faruk Celik, an AKP government minister in attendance at a conference held "for

---

5.   Merley, *Turkey, the Global Muslim Brotherhood, and the Gaza Flotilla* pp. 75-77.

6.   Merley, *Turkey, the Global Muslim Brotherhood, and the Gaza Flotilla* pp. 10, 20, 37.

the sake of Palestine," publicly expressed support for "the ship IHH intends to send to the Gaza Strip."

Though capable of ferrying over a thousand passengers, the Turkish vessel at the head of the flotilla, the *Mavi Marmara*, was sold to IHH for only $1.15 million by the AKP-controlled Istanbul City Municipality Transportation Corporation. Recall from our earlier discussion of IHH's ties to AKP that Ali Yandir, the senior manager of this transportation bureau, just happens to be an IHH trustee.[7]

Less than a week before the flotilla's launch, IHH vice president Yavuz Dede convened an organizers' conference in Istanbul. Minutes of the meeting, later found on a laptop aboard the *Mavi Marmara*, stated that, though Erdogan's "Government did not announce openly support for the mission at first," flotilla organizers "in the last few days [were] getting direct support from PM [i.e., Prime Minister Erdogan] and other ministers." Organizers were also advised, in discussions described as "f2f" (i.e., face-to-face), that "if we have any difficulties, gov [i.e., the government] will extend what support they can."[8]

Besides supplying a vessel for the flotilla, the Istanbul transportation bureau provided IHH with support that was even more crucial. As the AKP governmental entity responsible for operation of Turkey's ports, it is charged with carrying out required inspections. Most of the 500 Turkish citizens who participated in the flotilla were subjected to full, customary inspection upon boarding the *Mavi*

---

7. The boat was sold to IHH by a company called IDO (Istanbul Deniz Otobusleri—the Istanbul Sea Bus Company), which is owned by the Istanbul City Municipality Transportation Corporation, for 1.8 million Turkish lira (about $1.15 million). The Turkish newspaper *Aydnik* reported that IDO insisted on selling the boat at a loss. According to the Israeli Intelligence and Terrorism Information Center, a computer file later recovered from the boat discussed the IHH purchase of the Mavi Marmara from IDO.

8. Yaakov Katz, "Erdogan and Turkish Government Supported IHH" (*Jerusalem Post*, Jan. 24, 2011); see also Merley, *Turkey, the Global Muslim Brotherhood, and the Gaza Flotilla* pp. 10, 20, 37; *IHH Preparations for a Violent Confrontation with IDF Soldiers Aboard the Turkish Ship Mavi Marmara* (Aug. 6, 2010).

Marmara in the port of Antalya on May 26. Days earlier in Istanbul, however, forty voyagers were permitted to board the ship without inspection, along with the *Mavi Marmara's* twenty-nine crew members.

These forty were hardcore IHH operatives under the direction of Yildirim. They included Osman Atalay, the aforementioned IHH founder and Bosnian jihad veteran. The forty formed a disciplined group, according to an officer of the ship crew: setting up a situation room for IHH coordination; posting guards at passageways to prevent ordinary passengers from reaching the upper decks, which the IHH operatives controlled. Many of them had walkie-talkies, and some wore stickers identifying them as *Khares Amni*—"security protection." Their luggage included flares, night-vision goggles, 150 bulletproof vests and 200 gas masks, as well as several dozen slingshots. Some weapons were brought along and many others were collected or improvised onboard the *Mavi Marmara*. The eventual arsenal was found to include 200 knives, twenty axes, fifty wooden clubs, paint rollers from which sponges had been removed (the better to be used as weapons), and 100 assorted iron bars, metal shafts, and metal cables sawed off from the ship's railings.

There was a well publicized reception before the *Mavi Marmara* shoved off from Istanbul to pick up the other Turkish passengers in Antalya, after which the boat would cruise on to Cyprus to meet up with the flotilla's five other ships. At the Istanbul festivities, Yildirim made a point of thanking AKP for its support, while Seracettin Karayagiz, an AKP parliamentarian, exclaimed, "The Israeli weapons cannot be more powerful than human determination. Israel kills a thousand people, and after that they stand up and claim there is Islamic terrorism. We can't accept that."

Prime Minister Erdogan could have stopped the flotilla's Turkish contingent—at least, the IHH operatives who were patently spoiling for a fight. The Israeli government implored its counterparts in the AKP government, at very high ministry levels, to prevent the flotilla from departing, with the understanding that arrangements would be made to transport any real humanitarian aid into Gaza. Yet, the AKP did not merely decline to impede IHH; Erdogan's government abetted the operation.

It did so knowing full well that there would inevitably be a confrontation with the Israeli Defense Forces. In fact, while Erdogan's minions were encouraging the IHH agitators, Turkey's intelligence agency discouraged several AKP Parliament members from joining the voyage, as they'd hoped to do. The AKP wanted both strategic success and deniability: to provoke an altercation, to lure Israel into a no-win trap of either abandoning the blockade or being roundly condemned for defending it; but to do so with a minimum of graphic proof that Erdogan had orchestrated a forcible challenge to the blockade—an act of war.

As the fleet neared Gaza, there was chanting on the *Mavi Marmara*: "*Khaybar, Khaybar, ya Yahud, Jaish Muhammad saya'ud*"— meaning, "Oh Jews, remember Khaybar; the army of Mohammed is returning!" This chant was an allusion to a seventh-century massacre and expulsion by Muslims of a Jewish tribe in Khaybar, a town in what today is Saudi Arabia. Palestinian news carried reports of a woman passenger asserting, "We await one of two good things: to achieve martyrdom or to reach the shore of Gaza."

Late on the night of May 30, with the flotilla within a hundred nautical miles of Gaza, the Israeli navy verbally admonished the ships that they were approaching "an area of hostility which is under a naval blockade." The announcement emphasized that "the Israeli government supports delivery of humanitarian supplies to the civilian population of the Gaza Strip." The navy thus invited the flotilla to divert course and enter Israel's Ashod Port. There, any authentic humanitarian aid would be inspected and then transferred into Gaza "through formal land crossings." Flotilla passengers were assured that they would be allowed to observe the inspection, after which they could safely head back home.

The flotilla ignored these entreaties and kept provocatively advancing. In the early morning hours of May 31, with the flotilla now seventy nautical miles from the coast, Israeli navy vessels approached. IDF personnel were able to board five of the six ships, whose pro-Palestinian activists, having made their point, offered little resistance.

Things were very different on the *Mavi Marmara*. IHH operatives prepared for battle: donning their vests and masks, readying their weapons, and denying to non-combatant passengers any access to the main deck—which was strewn with bolts and screws to make for unsure footing when IDF forces came aboard. Pursuant to Yildirm's instructions, IHH operatives were to prevent IDF personnel getting on the ship, and to throw into the sea any who did manage to land.

At about 4:30 a.m., commandos aboard Israeli speedboats attempted to board the *Mavi Marmara*, but their grappling hooks were thrown back at them by IHH operatives. Minutes later, the IDF deployed helicopters from which commandos rappelled down to the ship, using three "flash bang" stun grenades, but no gunfire, to facilitate their descent. Hoping a show of force would allow them to take the ship without causing any loss of life, the commandos were primarily armed with paint-ball guns. They also carried side-arms loaded with live ammunition for use only if self-defense required it.

When they began landing on the deck, they were shot at and savagely beaten by IHH operatives wielding clubs, knives, and slingshots. One Israeli participant in the raid provided this chilling account:

> My commander was the first soldier that rappelled down from
> the helicopter to the ship. When he touched ground, he got
> hit in the head with a pole and stabbed in the stomach with a
> knife. When he drew out his secondary weapon—a handgun
> (his primary weapon was a regular paintball gun: "Tippman 98

SPRING FEVER

custom")—he was shot in the leg. He managed to fire a single shot before he was tossed from the balcony by Arab activists, to the lower deck (a 12 feet fall).

He was then dragged by other activists to a room in the lower deck were he was stripped down by 2 activists. They took off his vest, helmet and shirt, leaving him with only his pants and shoes on. When they finished they took a knife and expanded the wound he already had in his stomach. They cut his ab muscles horizontally and by hand spilled his guts out. When they finished they raised him up and walked him on the deck outside. He was conscious the whole time ... They wanted to show the soldiers their commander's body so they will be demoralized and scared.

Luckily, when they walked him on the deck a soldier saw him and managed to shoot the activist that was walking him down the outside corridor. He shot him with a special non-lethal bullet that didn't kill him. My commander managed to jump from the deck to the water and swim to an army rescue boat (his guts still out of his body, and now in salty sea water). That was how he was saved. The activists that did this to him are alive, now in Turkey, and treated as heroes.

As powerfully illustrated by both video recordings of the raid and eyewitness accounts, the Israeli commandos returned live fire only after the Islamist operatives attacked with lethal force. In the exchange, nine Israeli soldiers were wounded, including two who were shot. Nine members of the IHH contingent were killed, and a total of fifty-five other passengers were injured to one degree or another in the melee.

Erdogan pounced. He raced home from a Latin American junket to issue a firebreathing public condemnation. "Israel cannot clean the blood off its hands through any excuse," he railed. "It is no longer possible to cover up or ignore Israel's lawlessness. This bloody massacre by Israel on ships that were taking humanitarian aid to Gaza deserves every kind of curse." The flotilla incident, he added was a "turning point." The Israelis "once again showed their ability to perpetrate slaughters," and should "absolutely be punished by all means."

For his part, Sheikh Qaradawi inveighed against the "barbaric and unexpected crime" in which "the Zionist gang . . . attack[ed] activists and volunteers on board a defenseless ship." He hailed the "great Turkish stand" in defense of the Palestinian cause, a brand of heroism, he said, that put Arab countries to shame by comparison. The sheikh later issued a statement, co-signed by Rashid Ghannouchi and several other prominent Muslim Brotherhood figures, urging individual Muslims and Islamic countries to show their appreciation to Turkey by favoring it with tourism and trade.[9]

HAMAS'S SUGAR-DADDY: IT'S JUST POLITICS, NOT TERRORISM

Upon their return to Turkey, the IHH flotilla jihadists were received as heroes by the Erdogan government. Their plane was personally met by Deputy Prime Minister Bulent Arinc, and the wounded "humanitarians" were subsequently visited by Foreign Minister Ahmet Davutoglu and by Erdogan himself. Photos of Erdogan being embraced and kissed circulated throughout the Islamic media.

The prime minister was just getting started. He threatened future Gaza flotillas would be accompanied by the Turkish navy, raising the specter of firefight on the high seas between Jerusalem and Ankara's formerly allied naval forces, to say nothing of a broader regional war.

In championing Hamas's case to the U.N. panel that probed the *Mavi Marmara* raid, Erdogan's government insisted that the ship's passengers were mere humanitarian activists illegally confronted in neutral, international waters by an Israeli government seeking to vin-

---

9. Merley, *Turkey, the Global Muslim Brotherhood, and the Gaza Flotilla* pp. 90-94.

dicate an illegal blockade of sovereign Gaza. This was a remarkable argument in light of Turkey's own aggression in Cyprus. As Daniel Pipes points out, since invading Cyprus and terrorizing Greek Cypriots in the mid-Seventies, Turkey has effectively annexed the northern third of the country—occupying it with 30,000 troops and purporting to establish the "Turkish Republic of Northern Cyprus" (which no country other than Turkey recognizes). It has walled the occupied territory off from the rest of Cyprus, even as it condemns Israel's sealing of the Gaza border. While dismissing Israel's right to act in international waters to protect its own citizens and coastline from guaranteed terrorist attack, Turkey has threatened to use its own navy against Cyprus if it attempts to conduct oil exploration in international waters—especially if the drilling is in cooperation with Israel.

As we've noted, the U.N. panel rejected Turkey's contention that Israel's blockade violates international law, citing the well-known Hamas terrorist threat. Erdogan reacted bitterly. To the cheers of Islamic supremacists across the globe, the AKP government has conclusively ended all military ties to Israel. On the two-year anniversary of the flotilla incident, the regime's prosecutors filed an indictment against four Israeli commanders involved in the raid, seeking multiple life sentences—ranging from 8,000 to 18,000 years' of imprisonment—based on the discredited theory, popular in Islamist circles, that Israel has no right of self-defense.

In 2011, moreover, Erdogan, made a startling pronouncement on Charlie Rose's PBS program: "Let me give you a very clear message. I don't see Hamas as a terror organization. Hamas is a political party. And it is an organization. It is a resistance movement trying to protect its country under occupation. So we should not mix terrorist organizations with such an organization." Erdogan has since hosted Hamas's leaders—both Ismail Haniyeh and Khaled Meshaal—on separate occasions in Ankara. And in late 2011, a website belonging to Sheikh Qaradawi's terrorist organization, the Union for Good, was ecstatic to announce the news that Erdogan had directed his finance ministry to donate $300 million to the government of Gaza. That is to say, Turkey is now bankrolling Hamas. Erdogan has taken his country from NATO ally to terror sponsor.

CHAPTER ELEVEN

The Neo~Ottomans

It did not happen overnight. At the turn of the century, Turkey was still a bulwark of secularism, a close ally of Israel, and a friend of the West. A dozen years later, it is an Islamist champion of both violent jihadists pledged to annihilate Israel and Sunni supremacists engaged in a self-described "grand jihad" to destroy the West by sabotage.

While things were clearly changing by the mid- to late-Nineties, when Necmettin Erbakan was elected prime minister (then quickly cashiered in the "Postmodern Coup"), the real transformation occurred during the last decade. Recep Tayyip Erdogan's patient plan was ingeniously gradualist . . . because it had to be. And it has succeeded despite the unique advantages non-Arab, Eurocentric, and vigorously secular Turkey had for resisting the Islamist onslaught. Thus we can see why it hasn't taken nearly as long for today's "Arab Spring" to augur freedom's cold, dark winter.

TAMING THE GENERALS: "DEMOCRACY" DESTROYS DEMOCRACY

As in contemporary Egypt, the most formidable challenge for Turkey's Islamists was the military. But unlike the situation in contemporary Egypt, Turkey's military was not rife with Islamists. Erdogan had a much tougher nut to crack: an army that was adamantly Kemalist, secular, and proud of its modern, Western orientation, especially its membership in NATO. The Turkish military was inside the West's club, in a way the Turkish political class, pathetically pleading for European integration, would never be.

Times, though, were changing. As the Cold War receded, the United States and Europe grew less appreciative of alliances that were predominantly military in character and value. Western politicians became gratingly pious about the virtues of civilian governance and control over military commanders—regardless of the conditions inside particular countries. As we've seen, Erdogan could sense this even as he was carted off to jail during the "Postmodern Coup." Yes, the generals shoved Erbakan aside, but the shifting political sands left them too timid to take firm control of the government as they had done in the past.

By the mid-Nineties, when the latest Islamist surge began, Turkey was already lobbying for EU accession. Eurocrats emphasized the military's constitutional checkmate on Turkey's political order as an indelible stain on Ankara's petition. Concurrently, the United States came to be governed by a series of administrations, from both political parties, whose transnational-progressive foreign policy took seriously the slanders of America-bashers, particularly the absurd trope that America was "at war with Islam."

Having made this first error of allowing our nation to be defined by our enemies, our government inexorably fell into the next logical error: the frantic search for Islamic governments with which to align. No matter how energetically such governments worked against American interests, such alliances, we told ourselves, would convince "the Muslim world" that we really are lovable. In such a strange climate, the standing of Turkey's pro-American armed forces as a bulwark against resurgent Islamic supremacism was suddenly far less popular with America's ruling class.

Erdogan deftly exploited the climate to destroy that bulwark from within, the Muslim Brotherhood's signature strategy. Early in his first term, having only won a third of the popular vote and worried that the deep state might oust him just as it had ousted Erbakan, Erdogan largely steered clear of the generals. The prime minister strategically basked in European and American paeans to the democratic values of civilian supremacy and religious liberty, but otherwise bided his time: infiltrating his allies into the judiciary, intelligence services, and the military itself.

Finally, in the summer of 2006, an opportunity arose. On the horizon was the next year's election for the presidency—not an unimportant position but subservient to Parliament under Turkey's current constitution. Erdogan indicated his intention to have his old friend and ally Abdullah Gul stand as the AKP candidate. Gul was then serving Erdogan well. As foreign minister, he was responsible for steering Turkey's ostensible European integration effort: it was he prodding the Eurocrats who, in turn, obligingly warned Turkey's generals against interference in politics.

The military was peeved at the notion of a Gul presidency, which would give Islamists a lock on all of the government's most significant and visible political offices. Consequently, General Yasar Buyukanit, the hardline Kemalist military chief, posted what was dubbed the "E-Memo Warning" (*E-Muhtira*) on the General Staff's website, emphasizing the core principle of secularism and implicitly threatening a coup if Gul were to run and win.

With the economy doing well and his tenure globally praised as a time of political stability, Erdogan decided to call the military's bluff. He dissolved Parliament so that early elections could be held. As he expected, the AKP easily prevailed, nearly capturing half the popular vote (46.6 percent). Gul was sworn in as president and the chastened generals did nothing in response. With the stakes high, Erdogan had rolled the dice and won; politically speaking, the military had been exposed as a spent force. Clearly, the deep state was in retreat, and the prime minister's Islamist fangs were now on full, vengeful display.

JUSTICE—"ISLAMIC DEMOCRACY" STYLE

Shortly after the election, an AKP government prosecutor very publicly accelerated a sweeping investigation of an alleged terrorist network, labeled "Ergenekon." This shadowy enterprise is depicted in the Islamist media as the dark force behind seemingly every criminal act in Turkey since the dusk of the Cold War. That includes the deep state's vicious operations against separatist Kurds, its reputed collaboration with criminal syndicates, and its elaborate spying on Islamists. As Gareth Jenkins recounts in an analytical essay published by the *Middle East Review of International Affairs*, the pro-AKP press has sedulously fanned the flames, based on illegal government leaks (*torrents* would be a better word), to sear Ergenekon on the public consciousness as "synonymous with the deep state."

The only problem is: There's no there there. Ergenekon is a monstrous ruse, a transparent vehicle for arresting, imprisoning, harassing, and intimidating the regime's political critics and adversaries. Jenkins shows that among the hundreds detained are "university rectors, lawyers, journalists, television presenters, the author of some erotic novels, retired generals, the head of the Ankara Chamber of Commerce, and even Turhan Comez, a dissident former parliamentary deputy from the [AKP] who had resigned in 2007 in protest [over . . .] Erdogan's authoritarian management style."

The regime's prosecutors have filed thousands of pages of allegations—a single indictment, charging eighty-six people in 2008, is *2,445 pages long.* They accuse suspects of membership in "an armed terrorist organization" and of "inciting people to the armed rebellion against the government of the Turkish Republic." On close scrutiny, however, the charging instruments are incoherent, shot through with anachronisms and internal inconsistencies. They do not establish that such a thing as Ergenekon even existed, much less that the legions of accused defendants actually joined the fanciful conspiracy, which purportedly sought to control every terrorist organization not only in Turkey but in *the world*—and the indictments keep coming, so the eventual inclusion of outer space can't be ruled out.

If I were writing this in Turkey, I'd likely need to complete the next chapter in a jail cell. As Kemal Kulicdaroglu, the leader of AKP's main opposition wrote in a 2012 *Washington Post* op-ed, "The AKP is systematic and ruthless in its persecution of any opposition to its policies. Authoritarian pressure methods such as heavy tax fines and illegal videotaping and phone tapping are widely used to silence opponents." For criticizing the judges and prosecutors of this "Islamic democracy," Kulicdaroglu, naturally, became the subject of a criminal investigation.

Journalists and commentators who have the temerity to question the trumped up cases are subjected to Islamist smear campaigns until, finally, they are detained as enemies of the state and charged in the next round of indictments with membership in Ergenekon. In the "Islamic democracy" of Turkey, steered by the "moderate," "mildly Islamist" AKP, 95 journalists are currently imprisoned, some sentenced to as much as 166 years in the slammer, others staring at scores of charges that could result in sentences running into the *thousands* of years.

The persecution of reporters illustrates not only the innate authoritarianism of Islamist governance, but also Erdogan's lack of genuine interest in European integration. The latter was little more than a ploy to emasculate the Turkish military. "Western intellectuals," he scoffs, "have never experienced" a situation in which "journalists . . . take part in coups." Yes, of course: after all, what choice does a "democratic" leader have when faced with the totally unprecedented challenge of media scrutiny but to disappear his detractors?

It is a rout. Thoroughly cowed, the armed forces attempted no reprisals when a number of retired officers were rounded up in the initial stages of Ergenekon. An emboldened Erdogan publicly challenged the military, refusing to approve promotions either for generals implicated in Ergenekon or for General Aslan Guner—the secularist officer who had famously refused to shake hands with President Gul's wife because she wearing an Islamic headscarf (a kerfuffle discussed in Chapter 8). After a widely publicized standoff over this civilian interference in the military sphere, the house-broken generals again backed down.

With his secular opposition defenseless and reeling, Erdogan moved in for the kill: Down came a new round of indictments in 2010, stemming from a sedition investigation tellingly called "Sledgehammer." Scores of military officers have been detained in what is alleged to be a massive plot to stage a coup against the civilian government back in 2003—seven years earlier. Yet again, to call the evidence "dubious" would be generous.

CULTURAL ISLAMIZATION

In sum, Turkey is dhimmifying, a liminal phase in the transformational process of Islamization. Not only has the military been nullified as guardian of what should now be called the *former* secular order; Erdogan's control of the domestic security and intelligence apparatus has stratified Turkish society. Islamists who are loyal to the Sunni supremacist regime are safe; Kemalists, inquiring reporters, journalistic detractors, old-guard army officers, and authentic democrats, by contrast, quake in peril of trumped up indictments followed by lengthy detention while awaiting trial before a judicial bench increasingly staffed by AKP apparatchiks.

More significant even than the abuse of legal process is the resulting climate and its accelerant-effect on the real ballgame:

cultural Islamization. When the law devolves from a dispassionate refuge to an ideological weapon, Islamic supremacists know they have a wide berth to press their advantage. AKP needn't worry about formally enacting sharia-conforming laws, which would expose Erdogan as a democratic poseur. On the streets and in the expanding Islamist enclaves, sharia norms are being inculcated and enforced informally.

It is perverse to regard the Islamist AKP as a "model for the Arab Spring." As ruefully observed by Kemal Kulicdaroglu, the Turkish opposition leader, "Our democracy is regressing in terms of the separation of powers, basic human rights and freedoms and social development and justice." That is why, he concludes, Turkey scores "quite low in terms of human rights, democracy, freedoms and equality" in most major international indexes. He's right: the Middle East Forum's Aymenn Jawad al-Tamimi reports that in 2009, "Turkey dropped twenty places in Reporters Without Borders' "Press Freedom Index," to 122nd out of 175 countries. . . . In addition, the number of wiretapped phone calls, primarily against political opponents, has grown by around 50 percent annually since 2007, to a figure of 142,135 in 2009."

CALIPHATE IN THE MAKING

Concurrently, Erdogan moves full speed ahead to make Turkey a distinctly and aggressively Islamist presence on the world stage. Often, he is ostentatious, as we have seen in his stalwart support of Hamas and his undisguised contempt for Israel. But the groundwork for such strategically provocative displays has been laid by his signature caginess.

Largely unnoticed but vital to Erdogan's Islamist campaign is his profound influence over the Organization of Islamic Cooperation—formerly, the Organization of the Islamic Conference. The OIC consists of fifty-six countries plus the Palestinian authority (deemed by OIC members to be a sovereign state). Another Muslim

Brotherhood brainchild made possible by Saudi funding, the OIC primarily seeks global recognition of the worldwide ummah as a single, supranational community, with the OIC as its sovereign and voice. It is well on the way to achieving that goal. Indeed, every time the ubiquitous expression "the Muslim world" trips off our tongues, implicitly undermining the Western order of sovereign nation-states on which global relations have been based for centuries, we endorse the OIC's aspirations, wittingly or not.

Free people have no business encouraging such aspirations. The OIC's overarching aim is to Islamize societies through the gradual implementation of sharia standards. It would govern its subjects in accordance with classical sharia. It would also dramatically expand its domain beyond OIC countries by purporting to speak for Muslims *living in the West*. This is in accordance with supremacist ideology, which holds that a Muslim's fidelity is to the ummah, not to his home country. Recall Sheikh Qaradawi's "voluntary apartheid" approach to immigration: exhorting Muslims to integrate and multiply in the West but live in Islamic enclaves. Recall Erdogan's forceful condemnation of Western calls for Muslim assimilation as a "crime against humanity."

The OIC also prioritizes the elimination of Israel. As its 2005 "Ten-Year Progamme of Action" explains, it would first render the Jewish state indefensible by coercing its withdrawal to the 1967 borders—an objective Erdogan's friend and confidant, President Obama, has echoed. The OIC would then effectively bring about Israel's demise by compelling its acquiescence in all Palestinian demands, including: the establishment of "Palestine" as a nation with "al-Quds al-Sharif" (Jerusalem) as its capital; "counter[ing] the judaization [sic] of the Holy City"; and the granting of "inalienable Palestinian rights"—a transparent reference to the "right of return" by which millions of Palestinians would resettle in Israel. The latter attempt at demographic sea-change is an iteration of the "one state solution," in which the trendy conflation of popular elections with "democracy" would eviscerate Israel's character as a Jewish state.

The OIC's diplomatic campaign against Israel is willfully leveraged by violent jihad. It is noteworthy that, to this day, there is no internationally agreed upon definition of *terrorism*. Efforts in this regard have been stymied by the OIC, which insists that any U.N. definition must exclude "the activities of the parties during an armed conflict, including in situations of foreign occupation." The patent objective of this demand is to immunize Hamas in its anti-Zionist jihad. This is precisely why Erdogan and the OIC insist that Hamas is not a terrorist organization but a "resistance movement trying to protect its country under occupation."

There is a good reason why Turkey and the OIC are in such harmony. Thanks to heavy lobbying efforts by Erdogan and the AKP, Ekmeleddin Ihsanoglu, a Turkish academic, has been the OIC's secretary general since 2005. Professor Ihsanoglu is extremely useful in rallying Islamic countries and Muslim Brotherhood organizations, with which the OIC works closely, to Erdogan's imperatives: the legitimation of Hamas and de-legitimation of Israel, and the campaign not merely to smear criticism of Islam as "Islamophobia" but to criminalize it as defamation.

To take just one example of banging the Islamophobia drum, the OIC donated $325,000 in 2007 to a project jointly run by CAIR (an unindicted coconspirator in a then-ongoing Hamas financing prosecution) and Georgetown University's "His Royal Highness Prince Alwaleed bin Talal Center for Muslim-Christian Understanding" (established by $20 million in funding from the eponymous Saudi royal whose kingdom bans the practice of Christianity). The splashy conference Ihsanoglu hoped for did not pan out, but the propaganda campaign is still a smashing success: As this is written, the Obama administration, in consultation with its Islamist advisers, is purging training materials used by our military, intelligence and law-enforcement agencies of any information deemed offensive to Muslim sensibilities—anything, for example, suggestive of the nutty idea that a mainstream construction of Islamic scripture encourages jihadist violence . . . which is to say, anything that we federal prosecutors used to call "evidence" back in those bad old Islamophobic days of the Clinton Justice Department.

As a caliphate in the making, the OIC is also extraordinarily useful in enhancing the standing of Turkey (home of the last caliphate) and its prime minister. At the urging of Ihsanoglu, for example, Erdogan was honored by Saudi Arabia, center of the ummah's universe, with the 2010 "King Faisal International Prize" for "services to Islam," the OIC's version of the Nobel prize.

The next year, the OIC launched a campaign to drum up aid for drought-stricken Somalia—a hotbed of jihadist violence and Islamist aggression. The platform enabled Erdogan to ring the chimes of Western progressives with a *Foreign Policy* magazine op-ed in which he claimed terrorism by Somali Muslims—which, of course, has nothing to do with Islam—is the effect, rather than the cause, of "social instability, lawlessness and chaos." Meanwhile, back home in Istanbul, the prime minister resumed his more fiery pose, castigating the West as a civilization depraved by capitalism, "making trillions of dollars" while 3.7 million Somalis starve. The performance was choreographed as the catalyst spurring OIC countries to pony up $350 million for Somalia, further burnishing Erdogan's caliph credentials.

OUR NATO "ALLY'S" CIVILIZATION JIHAD

These are best burnished, though, by facing down the West with impunity. Indeed, by inducing the West to accede to Islamist demands. In classic Brotherhood style, the wily prime minister has masterfully pulled this off through a combination of gradualism and dissimulation. Erdogan has executed an Islamic supremacist foreign policy, "Neo-Ottomanism," under the guise of a congenial foreign policy the AKP labeled "Zero Problems with Neighbors"—reminiscent of the Brotherhood's rapacious "civilization jihad," which is pursued under such amiable banners as "Interfaith Understanding" and the "Alliance of Civilizations." Moreover, Erdogan has become more confrontational as his position improved over time: like the Turkish military, the West offers no resistance and each provocation makes Erdogan stronger.

"Zero Problems with Neighbors" arose out of Turkey's determination to cause enormous problems for its neighbor, Israel. As Erdogan methodically shred the Kemalist alliance with the Jewish state, he sought more cordial relations with Syria and Israel's Islamist enemies. Fully grasping that his course would nettle Turkey's NATO allies, Erdogan and his AKP foreign minister, Ahmet Davutoglu, dreamed up "Zero Problems" as the benign diplomatic packaging for this malicious shift.

Knowing the West's foreign policy solons just like a trainer knows his pets, Erdogan realizes there are two siren songs they find irresistible. The first is, "Let's negotiate." To our bright-lights, talking is always virtuous in and of itself. Negotiations can give temporizing the appearance of action. In the progressive mind, negotiations never legitimize bad actors, never give rogues the time and space needed to carry out some harmful plan, and never convey to malevolent states that the negotiator has no stomach for anything but talk, talk, talk.

The second bit of catnip is the long-craved Islamic "honest broker": that elusive Muslim government that will enjoy cordial relations with both Israel and Israel's enemies. Transnational progressives see this as the instrument needed to settle the Israeli-Palestinian conflict, which, as they figure everyone must know, is caused by mutual misunderstanding and the disputants' failure to negotiate—not by the incorrigible refusal of Muslim supremacists to accept Israel's existence.

If you follow this logic, you see that Turkey is not really hostile to Israel; it is just trying to be fair to both sides, to be the agent that can bring them together. We need that because, once the Islamic honest broker influences Israelis and Palestinians to end the "cycle of violence" and settle their "differences" in good faith, the end of this conflict will mean the end of all the West's problems in the region—because, as everyone must also know, if it weren't for Israel, Iran would not want nukes, Pakistan would not have nukes, Syria and Hezbollah would not control Lebanon, Muslim countries would not persecute Christians and other religious minorities, Sunnis and Shiites would not kill each other, and al Qaeda would not mass-murder Americans. Turkey, the silver bullet.

Thus did Erdogan sell "Zero Problems" to Bush, Obama, Europe, and Israel. It is a cover story for the pursuit of Turkey's real objective: transition from the Western to the Islamic sphere. Erdogan makes mischief and earns the ummah's adulation, while Western chancelleries convince themselves that he is helping them conduct "outreach," "build bridges," and prove that Islam and democracy really are compatible—the perfect recipe for global security and prosperity. In fact, "Zero Problems with Neighbors" is even vaguely reminiscent of Ataturk's "Peace at Home, Peace Abroad" policy . . . except for the small detail that the Kemalists were shifting *Westward*.

Zero Problems enabled Erdogan to strike a long-term strategic partnership with the Assad regime. This maneuver just happened to coincide with yet another "Arab Spring," the 2005 Cedar Revolution in Lebanon, where Assad's vice grip was being threatened by international ire over the murder of Prime Minister Rafic Hariri. Western intelligence sources and the early phase of a U.N. investigation pegged the homicide as a joint venture between Syria and Hezbollah. The West seized the moment of acrimony against Syria to push for—*all together now!*—"democracy" in Lebanon . . . the kind of "democracy" in which Hezbollah, having rubbed out its chief competitor, gets to run for election. As the American and French governments spearheaded this deft strategy, their model "Islamic democracy" ally, Turkey, threw its support to Assad, joining Iran as the only countries to do so.

Does it get any better? When the dust settled, Syria got away with the Hariri murder unscathed, while Hezbollah achieved "democratic" legitimacy, winning a sizable bloc of parliamentary seats and government ministries. Thanks to the elections so breathlessly celebrated in America and Europe, Hezbollah operatives now appear as government dignitaries when they attend Muslim Brotherhood confabs in Istanbul. And of course, it is now much more difficult for the United States to ostracize Hezbollah as a murderous terrorist organization. After all, as our key ally Erdogan maintains, Muslim "resistance" and "political" organizations must not be confused with "terrorists"—a term we should reserve for Israelis. Through the alchemy of "Islamic Democracy," the Iranian-backed Lebanese jihadists are now a "political" movement, and it has become an Obama administration priority to promote what the president's top national security adviser, John Brennan, calls Hezbollah's "moderate elements."

Lately, there have been some curious sighs of relief in the West because Erdogan has decried Assad's brutal campaign to crush an internal revolt. But the chill in the romance is easily explained. Assad's main opposition is the Muslim Brotherhood. That is why Hamas recently abandoned its longtime Syrian aerie. This is not a case of Erdogan, having realized that Damascus is run by thugs after all, vectoring back toward Turkey's former, pro-Western opposition to Assad. He is simply siding with his fellow Sunni Islamists as they seek to topple their tormentors—a government of minority Alawites, a stray and unorthodox branch of Shia Islam, persecuting a population that, like Turkey, is overwhelmingly (74 percent) Sunni.

Perhaps the most perverse aspect of Zero Problems is Erdogan's cultivation of warm ties with Iran. Unlike Syria, Iran is a lopsidedly Shiite country—there is no substantial Sunni faction to challenge the regime or vie for Erdogan's loyalties. For an Islamist, the mullah-led theocracy is the only game in town, which is why Hamas and al

Qaeda, Sunni terror groups, have willingly collaborated with Iran for years. Now, Turkey does, too. As the credulous West nods, Erdogan rationalizes that Turkey shares with Iran both a border and testy relations with an unassimilated Kurdish minority—to say nothing of their mutual fondness for Hamas and Hezbollah.

The real takeaway for Western powers ought to be this: While they've been telling themselves that Sunnis and Shiites despise each other, Islamists of both stripes despise the West more. When a situation involves only Sunnis and Shiites, they will turn on each other, often savagely (Erdogan, for example, is now lining up with the Sunni minority in Iraq against the Shiite-dominated government). When the West intervenes, however, rival Islamic supremacists will put aside their differences and work against non-Muslims (see, e.g., Iran—with which Erdogan has lined up against NATO). It's very simple: the objective of Islamic supremacists is Islamization, not Western democracy.

Erdogan has brazenly embraced Iranian President Mahmud Ahmadinejad—who, when not hooking up with Turkey's prime minister for photo-ops and consultations about "the arrogance of the Western countries," is regularly found threatening to wipe Israel off the map and openly envisioning "a world without America" ("Death to America" being Iran's national slogan . . . and objective). Turkey has openly supported Iran's nuclear program, with Erdogan channeling the mullahs' risible claim that their nuclear quest is for peaceful civilian purposes. At some point, the prime minister and his hand-picked president, Abdullah Gul, may have to get their story straight: Gul has publicly conceded that "it is [Iran's] final aspiration to have a nuclear weapon in the end."

In the interim, Erdogan has confounded the West by opposing its bids to impose U.N. sanctions against the Islamic Republic. How can Turkey take this position (and several of its other positions) and still be welcome in NATO? The question would be puzzling were it not for the U.S. government's ownfecklessnesson Iran, coupled with our smitten President's goo-goo eyes for Erdogan and determination to court the Muslim Brotherhood.

Joining forces with Ahmadinejad and Assad against the West only scratches the surface of Erdogan's Islamization project. So does the prime minister's cultivation of ties with the genocidal Islamist regime in Sudan. Reminiscent of his bloviating defense of Yasin al-Qadi (discussed in Chapter 9), Erdogan has offered himself as a character witness for Sudanese President Omar al-Bashir, whose ethnic cleansing campaign in Darfur earned him an international war crimes indictment. But not to worry: Erdogan says Bashir must be innocent because "a Muslim can never commit genocide." Good to have that cleared up. Erdogan also took time out from a 2006 Arab League summit to huddle with another shadowy Sudanese Islamist, Dr. Fatih al-Hassanein. In collusion with the Muslim Brotherhood, al-Hassanein used an ostensible charity, the Third World Relief Agency, to funnel millions of dollars (mostly from Islamist governments in Saudi Arabia, Iran and Sudan) to jihadists in Bosnia and the Brotherhood's satellite in Sudan.

TARGETING THE FIRST AMENDMENT: THE "DEFAMATION" CANARD
None of it seems to matter. In Western esteem, the Erdogan star burns only brighter with each new affront. Fresh from a recent sharia triumph—removing homosexuals from the groups protected by a U.N. resolution against discriminatory violence—the OIC is once again ratcheting up pressure to criminalize speech that it construes as "defamation of religion," meaning any critical examination of Islam. The Obama administration is not only encouraging this gambit; it hosted a late 2011 OIC conference—a "High Level Meeting on Combating Religious Intolerance"—to move the effort forward.

The State Department hailed as a break-through the fact that the latest iteration of the proposal would outlaw not mere "defamation" but instead "incitement to imminent violence based on religion or belief." It is deluding itself. This distinction refers only to what is explicitly criminalized; the new resolution actually goes much further, condemning—even if it does not expressly call for criminalization of—"any advocacy of religious hatred" that could incite not only violence but even "discrimination" or "hostility." Incitement to violence is already a crime; there is no need for a resolution against it. Consequently, the real purpose of the proposal is clear: to move the United States away from the First Amendment and toward the sharia standard Islamists have intimidated Europe into adopting, under which casting Islam in an unfavorable light is deemed actionable "hate speech."

The plan is working. Contemporaneously with hosting the OIC, the Obama administration unveiled a new counterterrorism strategy that bleaches out all references to "Islam" in addressing terrorism committed by Islamic supremacists. This mindset, which now pervades the executive branch, very much including the Pentagon, has led to some tragically hilarious exchanges in congressional hearings, such as: Attorney General Holder's writhing refusal to concede that "radical Islam" may have something to do jihadist attacks; National Intelligence Director James Clapper's insistence that the Muslim Brotherhood is a "largely secular" group that "has eschewed violence"; and the testimony of Paul Stockton, the Defense Department's Assistant Secretary for Homeland Defense, who steadfastly declined to admit that "violent Islamist extremism" was a problem because "I don't believe it's helpful to frame our adversary as 'Islamic' with any set of qualifiers that we might add, because [*here it comes!*] we are not at war with Islam."

Meanwhile, as Erdogan encourages more flotillas to break Israel's blockade of Hamas, the West accedes to Turkey's demands that Israel be barred from participation in NATO meetings and exercises, and that the European Union be excluded from NATO summits unless the OIC—that would be Iran, "Palestine," Sudan, and the rest of the gang—is included.

OBAMA COUNTERTERRORISM: EXCLUDING ISRAEL AND "RESISTANCE"

And what has been President Obama's reaction to Neo-Ottomanism? To mark the tenth anniversary of the 9/11 atrocities, the administration invited Turkey, as the world's leading "Islamic democracy," to join the administration's "Global Counterterrorism Forum" as Washington's top partner. At the gala Waldorf Astoria launch on September 22, 2011, Secretary of State Hillary Clinton was effusive in praising "my friend and colleague, Turkish Foreign Minister Davutoglu, as co-chair. We know very well Turkey's commitment to strengthening international cooperation against the threats we all face. . . . So I thank you, Ahmet, for being here for this kick-off."

Mrs. Clinton went on to thank the administration's other valued friends in the fight against terrorism: Saudi Arabia, Egypt, the United Arab Emirates, and Russia." There were no thanks for Israel, though. Israel wasn't invited.

The Secretary of State then ticked off her list of terrorists, from "al Qaeda and its affiliates" to "other terrorist groups like the [Kurdistan Workers Party], Lashkar e-Tayyiba, the FARC." But there was no mention of Hamas, Hezbollah, or Palestinian Islamic Jihad, Turkey's preferred "resistance" movements.

Finally, our alliterative chief diplomat took time to deplore the slaughter of innocents from "London to Lahore, from Madrid to Mumbai, from Kabul to Kampala." Somehow, though, as my friend Diana West noted, Tel Aviv, Ashkelon, and Jerusalem—or is it al-Quds?—didn't make the cut.

Mr. Erdogan's train has left the station. Our government seems inclined to follow.

CHAPTER TWELVE

Spring Fever

"Parliamentarian democracy will never accept such decisions." Recep Tayyip Erdogan, prime minister of Turkey, prime mover of the Organization of Islamic Cooperation, and prime advocate of vacating the democracy train once it has been safely steered to sharia station, was venting his spleen over Egypt's ruling military junta.

It was June 2012 and history was repeating itself in Egypt. Finally given their druthers, Egyptians had voted overwhelmingly to be ruled by Islam. This was not a case of Muslims voting for Muslims out of the vague bond one feels with fellow believers—the way American Catholics were drawn to John F. Kennedy even if his politics were not exactly their politics. Nor was the vote an illustration of Egyptian belief in *Islam,the religion*. No, Egyptians had chosen, by a four-to-one margin, to be governed by unabashed Islamic supremacists whose stated objective—". . . the Koran is our law, jihad is our way . . ."—is to implement *Islam, the totalitarian social system*. In the warped common parlance, they had chosen "Islamic democracy." But now, the Supreme Council of the Armed Forces (SCAF) was assuming the spoiler's role that military commanders in Turkey traditionally played—or at least used to play before Erdogan vanquished them in the course of forging an "Islamic democracy."

SCAF, flexing its Mubarak-like muscles, had just announced that it was dissolving Parliament—technically, that it was enforcing a high court ruling that Parliament should be dissolved (for, like the high court in the former Kemalist deep state, the high court in Egypt is reliably responsive to the desires of the generals). The move would effectively undo the free elections trumpeted throughout the West as the crowning achievement of the "Arab Spring" . . . at least until it became impossible to continue making believe that friendly Facebook progressives, rather than virulently anti-Western zealots, would win going away. It was this SCAF dissolution decision that had Erdogan incensed.

The historic election five months earlier had been lopsided. Egypt, as we've seen, is not Turkey. Islamists are not a minority. To win, they did not need, as Turkey's AKP needed, to exploit a quirk in the electoral framework that was designed to keep them out of power. In Egypt, what kept the Islamists out of power were dictators and their armies, period. The world's most populous Arab Muslim country is the intellectual home of Sunni supremacism and the cradle of the Muslim Brotherhood. The Brothers have survived through decades of repression because they personify the Islam of the Egyptian mainstream.

In fact, the real story of the Parliamentary election was the "Salafist" parties—so-called to distinguish them from the Brotherhood, and make the Brotherhood appear comparatively moderate, even though the Brothers, too, are Salafists. For anyone who actually familiarized himself with Egypt rather than reading the Arab Spring fairy tale on offer from the Western press, the Brotherhood's easy victory was no surprise. The eye-opener was the Salafists' spectacular success. Democracy devotees had hoped that some secular wave would miraculously materialize and roll back the Brotherhood's support. (Ironic that secularists are always hoping for divine interven-tion!) Turned out it was the Salafists—more rabid than the cautious Brothers for rapid sharia upheaval—who managed to steal some of the Brothers' thunder. The quarter of the popular vote they won, combined with the half claimed by the Brotherhood, gave Islamic supremacists a whopping 75 percent stranglehold on the legislature, which would translate into tight control over the committee that would write a new Egyptian constitution.

And now, in early June, the decisive run-off round of the pres-idential election was only a few days away, and the Brotherhood appeared poised to capture that office, too. SCAF had engaged in no small amount of chicanery to block them—saber-rattling; trying to hold the Brothers to their early, mendacious pledge not to run a presidential candidate; banning popular Islamist candidates on dubious technicalities. All for naught: this was Egypt, and if you're going to have real popular elections in Egypt—if you're not going to rig them, even if you'll try everything short of rigging—Islamic supremacists are going to win.

So now the generals were scrambling, frantic to slam shut the Pandora's Box Western leaders, delirious with spring fever, had hec-tored them into opening. But SCAF, like the Turkish generals in the Postmodern Coup, lacked the nerve to act decisively: Parliament would be dissolved . . . but the presidential election would go ahead, anyway. Lawmakers would be locked out . . . but maybe they would still help write the new constitution, and maybe the lockout would be rescinded. The generals wanted everyone to know they were not staging a coup . . . they were just ensuring that "the people's will" in this predominantly fundamentalist, 90 percent Sunni Muslim country would not be too, er, willful.

Erdogan had seen this show before, with a Turkish army that couldn't make up its mind whether he should be crushed as a sedi-tionist gadfly or allowed to take over the government. His advice to the Muslim Brotherhood was simple: Stay strong: the generals are no match for the democracy fetishists—SCAF would wilt. "In a democracy, rules are clearly defined," Turkey's prime minister thundered. "Once you embark on that road, you cannot introduce new rules"—at least not until democracy has locked in sharia, at which point "that road" has reached its dead end.

ISLAM DEVOURS THE "FACEBOOK REVOLUTION"

Within days of Tunisian fruit vendor Mohammed Bouazizi's self-immolation on December 17, 2010, igniting angry demonstrations in Tunis against government corruption and economic hardship, all eyes were on Cairo. Yes, it was Tunisia where the uprising swiftly toppled the regime of President Zine el Abidine Ben Ali, who fled to Saudi Arabia a step or two ahead of the posse. But it was *Egypt*, the world's most populous Arab Muslim country, and its most important in the estimation of many, that stirred the imagination. *Time* magazine, that bellwether of trite media meme, was in full frisson at the prospect that Egypt "was about to have a Facebook Revolution."

But what about the Islamists, who had always been the very fabric of Egypt? Their day, one was led to believe, had come and gone. The reports of Bouazizi copycats in Cairo, the agitation erupting in Tahrir Square, epicenter of the revolt—these were sure signs of a new era, of young people galvanized not by anything as quaint as ideology but by the burning desire to live freely. They had no interest in sharia. They wanted economic prosperity. They wanted out from under the boot of the despot who had looted the treasury while the masses lived in squalor.

Did these excited young demonstrators really evince the hopes of Egyptian society? For a sliver of it, sure. And for a time, with the right images and media spin, a sliver of 80 million people can be made to look like a countrywide groundswell. Egypt, however, is a more complicated place.

Though predominantly Islamic, the country is home to about eight million non-Muslims, mostly Copts. Of the seventy million-plus Muslims, a very sizable segment is devout and fundamentalist, anti-Western, and supportive of sharia implementation. Yet even this contingent is not monolithic. As we've seen, there is in Islamic culture a docile current of submission to the authority of the state. That is particularly true in a state, such as Egypt, where sharia is formally regarded as governing law in the constitution, even if the dictators paid it little deference in practice. Consequently, while Islamist factions have for decades, with varying degrees of ardor, sought to supplant the regime with a true sharia government, for millions of other devout Egyptians, support for sharia did not necessarily translate into a desire to oust the dictator—especially if there was a chance that he'd be replaced with something even less sharia-compliant.

Adding to the mix, millions of Egyptian Muslims, like millions of Turkish Muslims, are not fundamentalists. They are "secular Muslims." That term may be regarded as oxymoronic in the Erdogan home or as apostasy in Qaradawi enclaves and around the campus at al-Azhar. Nonetheless, it reflects a real phenomenon: Muslims who regard sharia as, at most, a matter of private ethics, not a roadmap for public policy. That these Muslims are grossly outnumbered in Egypt and in the broader Middle East does not mean they don't exist. Some of them are strongly pro-Western, but a goodly number are anti-Western Leftists of a Nasserite bent.

The commentariat in the United States and Europe lauds diversity in the abstract, but it is not very interested in understanding diversity down here on earth, particularly in faraway places. As the Tahrir Square upheaval unfolded, "the Egyptian people" thus became the projection screen for whatever imaginary monolith comported with the particular commentator's policy preferences. When progressive democracy devotees looked at Egypt, they saw only the pro-Western secularists. Discounting profound cultural differences between Islam and the West, presuming instead that all people are essentially the same and have a common yearning for freedom, they marginalized Egyptians who did not fit the mold. It was as if these tens of millions were some unrepresentative fringe or the invention of unhinged Islamophobes—we lunatics who see "workplace violence" and immediately start thinking, "*Jihad!*"

On the other hand, many analysts who were justifiably alarmed over the potential Muslim Brotherhood ascendancy, portrayed the Brothers as if they were ten feet tall—poised to roll effortlessly over secular Egyptians, hijack the armed forces, and begin bombing Tel Aviv by noon tomorrow. Progressives, meantime, looked at Egyptian socialists and saw their kind of democracy, one in which coalitions with "moderate Islamists" would seamlessly form.

Egypt is more complex than these competing depictions allowed. The one thing it is not is democratic. The Sunni supremacists, who favor classical sharia governance, are a patent majority. Led by the Brotherhood, their great advantages are organization and discipline. Those can be the decisive edge in a fractious society, where suffocating dictatorship has stymied the development of potential democratic competitors—although, as the parliamentary election showed, the Muslim Brotherhood's main competition appears to come from the sharia side, not the democracy side.

Still, the military remains a formidable obstacle for the Islamists. It is, and has long been, the powerfully armed, expertly trained, lavishly financed backbone of the regime. In addition, it essentially controls what little productive industry Egypt has left—crony benefits it would not surrender without a fight. As we shall shortly see, Egypt's armed forces are not as formidable an obstacle for Islamists as was the Turkish military that Erdogan had to tame. But they are no push-over—especially when complemented by the various slices of Egyptian life that realize they have less to fear from a Mubarak-style police state than from sharia totalitarianism.

If there was one factor that united the disparate factions to demand Mubarak's ouster and that convinced the military to abandon him, it was not a yearning for either democracy or sharia. Nor was it revulsion over Mubarak's iron fist. Sure, that was what most aggrieved the Western press, which takes its cues from progressive intellectuals and self-styled human rights crusaders. Egypt, however, has long been wracked by jihadist terror, and while Islamists groused ceaselessly over the regime's periodic crackdowns, many Egyptians were glad for them.

No, what the vast majority of Egyptians had had their fill of after thirty years was not Mubarak's brutality but his cupidity. He and his family socked away a fortune larger than Egypt's prodigious public debt, making them billionaires many times over. And this, in a country with rampant poverty, real unemployment at over 20 percent, many working Egyptians surviving on only a few hundred dollars a year, and reserves sufficient to cover imports for, at most, a few months—meaning anxiety over hunger and looting looms large.

So Mubarak had to go, and go he did on February 11, 2011. This was an Egyptian decision and perhaps an inevitable one. Mubarak was substantially pro-American: an anti-jihadist and a staunch backer of the peace with Israel that his government has kept, despite widespread public opposition in Egypt, since the 1978 Camp David Accord.

THE "LARGELY SECULAR" MUSLIM BROTHERHOOD

Of course, the United States cannot control the internal affairs of other countries, no more than we can justly be blamed for the messes those countries make of themselves. We can, however, help or hurt our cause. When our vital interests are at stake, that is no small thing. In Egypt, Mubarak's pro-American policies were of great significance to us, even if Mubarak, himself, was not. Our interests lay in seeing those policies sustained. The very public Bush crusade for democracy at any cost (translation: popular elections), coupled with the Obama campaign to indulge Islamic grievances and romance the Muslim Brotherhood, have gravely imperiled those policies.

As Egypt unraveled, the Obama administration's performance was pure amateur hour. One day it backed Mubarak as an important ally, the next day support was tepid, the next day he had to go. President Obama reeled, topsy-turvy, with the drastic turns of events. He called for Mubarak's ouster only after Mubarak's ouster was unavoidable. By then, Brotherhood spokesmen were already braying that the Camp David peace could be terminated by a popular referendum, and that Egyptians "should be prepared for war against Israel."

The dictator's toppling brought to the fore the only question that really mattered: What happens next? Here, too, Obama was at sea. At the beginning, his administration did not seem to realize that the catastrophe of Islamist accession to power was inevitable. Back then, before Obama began to prepare the political ground for failure by perfuming the pig—i.e., by branding the Muslim Brotherhood as an agreeable, "largely secular" lot—the President did not quarrel with the contention that the Brothers were a huge problem for the West. Not to worry, though: they were, he insisted, a harmless minority faction. He concurred with his friend, the Leftist Egyptian politician Mohammed ElBaradei, that the Brotherhood appealed to a quarter or less of the population.

Nevertheless, even if one accepted the President's assessment for argument's sake, a plurality of that magnitude would be a fierce challenge. That is especially so when no one else has anything close and when, as an Alinskyite might notice, no other community is organized. The Bolsheviks probably had less popular support in 1917 than Obama figured the Brotherhood did in early 2011. And unlike the Bolsheviks, the Brothers had been preparing for their moment for eighty years. When it came, they were ready to hit the ground running.

From the moment Mubarak stepped down, dark omens about the trajectory of Egypt's emerging "Islamic democracy" began appearing. CBS news correspondent Lara Logan, in Tahrir Square to cover the frenzy when the dictator's fall was announced, was grabbed by a mob and gang-raped. To the shamefully limited extent the media, even CBS, covered the attack, the spin was that this sort of thing could have happened in any setting where raw emotion erupts—even, say, in Wisconsin, where the Left's union agitators were then protesting against Republican Governor Scott Walker.

Except it doesn't happen in Madison. It happens in Egypt. Just as it happened in Indonesia, the world's most populous Muslim country, in the riots that led to Suharto's fall. Rape is a staple of Islamic supremacism in Muslim countries and in the Muslim enclaves of Europe and Australia.[1] Enabled by the cowardly silence of the media, the rapists act on a sense of entitlement derived from their scriptures. That this is not the only way these scriptures can be construed is not a justification for ignoring how they are understood in the Middle East mainstream.

To understand why rape happens like this, one need only peruse the al-Azhar-endorsed sharia manual, *Reliance of the Traveller*, which we explored in Chapter 3. It is quite clear on the subject of women who become captives of Muslim forces: "When a child or a woman is taken captive, they become slaves by the fact of capture, and the woman's previous marriage is immediately annulled." This is so the woman can then be made a concubine of her captor. Such arrangements are encouraged by the Koran. Sura 4:23–24, for example, forbids Muslim men from consorting with the wives of other Muslims but declares sexual open season on any women these men have enslaved. ("Forbidden to you are . . . married women, except those whom you own as slaves.")

Indeed, the celebrated Brotherhood jurist Yusuf Qaradawi contends that women bring sexual abuse on themselves if they fail to conform to Islamist conventions of modest dress. If the barbaric treatment of Ms. Logan was not sufficient as a cautionary tale about where Sheikh Qaradawi's teachings lead, his own triumphant appearance in Tahrir Square surely was.

---

1. See McCarthy, *The Grand Jihad*, pp. 98-101.

143

With Mubarak out of the way and control of the revolution up for grabs, the Western media began assuring increasingly alarmed readers and viewers that there was little chance Egypt would go the way of Iran because the uprising lacked a Khomeini-like charismatic cleric to seize the moment. But then the Brotherhood began shunting aside non-Islamist opposition leaders, including the Google executive Wael Ghonim, whom Western media had posited as emblematic of the uprising's modernist, progressive character. After all, well over a million Muslims were not jamming the square to hear a good corporate citizen of the Left; they were there to hear Sheikh Qaradawi, sharia personified.

Just a week after Mubarak's expulsion, on Juma—i.e., Friday, the Islamic Sabbath, when the uprising tended to heat up as Muslims poured out of their mosques with the voices of fiery imams still ringing in their ears—Sheikh Qaradawi was cheered like a rock star in Tahrir Square. Tellingly, security for his appearance in the former backyard of his archenemy, Mubarak, was provided by the Egyptian military . . . even as the Brothers were preventing non-Islamist speakers from taking the podium. The Brothers and the generals, it seemed, could reach accommodations. In his sermon, Qaradawi celebrated the revolution as Allah's victory and heralded it as a divine omen for "our brothers in Palestine"—meaning Hamas. Just as Allah had provided "victory in Egypt," so too would there soon be a "conquest of the al-Aqsa Mosque" in Jerusalem.

DON'T BET ON THE EGYPTIAN MILITARY

Soon, murderous attacks against Coptic Christians intensified. On New Year's Eve, a church in Alexandria was bombed, killing twenty-three. In March, angry mobs attacked a Cairo church. In April, rioters in Qena demanded the ouster of the regime-appointed governor because he is a Christian and thus, under sharia, unfit to govern in a Muslim land. In May, screaming, "With our blood and soul, we will defend you, Islam!" jihadists stormed the Virgin Mary

Church in northwest Cairo, torched it, burned to the ground the nearby homes of two Copt families, attacked a residential complex, killed a dozen people, and wounded over 200 more. In October, thousands of Muslims attacked and destroyed the St. George Coptic church in Edfu. The pastor had been insufficiently attentive to their complaints that the renovation of the house of worship, carried out only after government approval, left it with a "cross [that] irritates Muslims and their children." And then there was that dome that made it look like, well, a church.

Flabbergasted that the world seemed indifferent to their plight, thousands of Copts went to Maspero, a Cairo media center, to draw attention. The demonstration turned into a shocking massacre when some soldiers opened fire on the protesters and others rammed cars into them. Dozens of Christians were killed and 300 wounded— though the media focused on the three soldiers who lost their lives in the melee started by the military. Video circulated of a soldier boasting that he had shot a Christian in the chest, after which the crowd around him shouted, "*Allahu Akbar!*"

The revolution was taking a decisive, predictably perilous, turn. Still, Western governments and commentators would not come to terms with what was happening, with what "Islamic democracy" was yielding.

The next reassuring talking point was: "Don't worry, the Egyptian military will never let the crazies take over." Those making this foolish claim lacked even an awareness of the present—of Prime Minister Erdogan's ongoing decimation of the westernized Turkish armed forces as a barrier to Islamization, or of the military's complicity in Egypt's rampant anti-Christian butchery. It stood to reason, then, that they would lack any sense of history.

"My name is Khalid Islambouli, I have slain Pharaoh, and I do not fear death!" Thus went the chilling exclamation at the annual military parade in Cairo on October 6, 1981. Lieutenant Islambouli, graduated as an officer after being a star student at the Egyptian

Military Academy, had just broken off from his march to strafe the reviewing stand with bullets. He had murdered President Anwar Sadat and hurtled his nation into chaos.

That was the plan. Islambouli, like several of his coconspirators, was a Muslim Brotherhood veteran who'd drunk deep the incitements of Sayyid Qutb. His patience exhausted by the Brotherhood's Fabian approach to revolution, he moved on to Egyptian Islamic Jihad, one of several splinter groups that would later be folded into al-Qaeda by another Brotherhood alum, Ayman al-Zawahiri. Islambouli had hoped to trigger an Islamic upheaval by "cutting off the head of the snake." But beyond murdering Sadat, the plan fizzled. Power passed seamlessly to Sadat's vice president, Hosni Mubarak, who crushed the jihadist coup attempt.

In that drama, one tie beyond citizenship united all the major players: the villain, the victim, the heroes who stanched the uprising, and the bureaucrat who ended up ruling Egypt for the next thirty years. They were all members of the Egyptian military.

It is Egypt's most stable institution and, with the possible exception of al-Azhar University, its most revered one. The army's professionalism has been purchased at a cost of nearly $40 billion from U.S. taxpayers since 1978, when Sadat made the peace with Israel that drove the jihadists to kill him. Commentators who highlight the military's stability, then, are implying that this heavy American investment, fortified by a generation of training and cooperative relations with America's unparalleled armed forces, is insurance on which the United States can depend for the protection of our interests. Don't bet on it. As a guardian against Islamic supremacism, Egypt's military is far less dependable than the Turkish military—the guys who couldn't get the job done. After all, Egypt's armed forces have never had that responsibility in the first place.

As the Turkish generals learned, military takeovers are now taboo. The democracy fetish won't allow for them. It matters not whether such a seizure of authority would be in patriotic good faith, to guard against totalitarian control of the state or to give the society a reasonable amount of time to try to build democratic culture and institutions. It matters not whether, as an objective matter, a military coup would be the best thing for the country as well as for regional stability.

Transnational progressives may not seem particularly impressed by the democratic value of self-determination when, say, the state of Texas upholds its death penalty provisions against the caterwauling of human rights activists. In those instances, we are lectured about the need to yield to enlightened international consensus. But when self-determination involves a country's choosing to be run by Islamic supremacists, then the Tranzies become champions of popular sovereignty: Islamic supremacists it must be. Indeed, after the Muslim Brotherhood began winning elections in Egypt, Secretary of State Hillary Clinton decreed that it was "imperative" for the armed forces to "turn power over to the legitimate winner."

Moreover, let's pretend coups had not become *declasse*, and that Egypt's armed forces, without inhibition, could act to thwart the Islamist surge. Would they? It is doubtful.

Lt. Islambouli's status as an officer is what enabled him to be assigned to the parade so he could kill Sadat. How, you may wonder, does a violent jihadist become a military officer and get close enough to kill the Egyptian president—at a time when it was well known that Camp David had made Sadat a marked man? Very simple: The Egyptian military is a reflection not of its American trainers but of Egyptian society at large. The Maspero massacre described above underscores this fact. The popularity of the armed forces owes in large part to the fact that almost all able-bodied men are conscripted to serve for one to three years. Its uppermost ranks, from which rose Egypt's presidents—Mubarak, Sadat, and modern Egypt's founder, Nasser—tend to be pro-American. The mid-level officers and the lower ranks, however, have always included thousands of Muslim fundamentalists.

Unlike Turkey, Egypt has never had a secularization project, much less, a thoroughgoing effort to purge Islam from public life, of the kind Kemalists attempted for the better part of a century—unsuccessfully, as it turned out. To be sure, military service is a leveling experience, creating a common bond that unites different social strata. We should not overstate its effect, though. In Egypt, the armed forces feature all the complexity and divisions of Egyptian society at large.

They have also always been more follower than leader. Nasser dragged the military from loyalty to the British-backed monarchy into the Soviet orbit. Sadat moved it into America's column. Under Mubarak, it has maintained a cold peace with Israel, but it would be naïve to think new leadership could not shift the military back to hostilities against a nation most Egyptians find repugnant—a nation with which Egypt fought four wars between 1948 and 1973.

In the past twenty years, two former Egyptian military officers have come to prominent attention in the United States. The first was Emad Salem, a pro-American Muslim, who volunteered to infiltrate the New York terror cell formed by the Blind Sheikh, Omar Abdel Rahman (Abdel Rahman, coincidentally, having issued the fatwa authorizing Sadat's murder before going on, incessantly, to call for the killing of Mubarak). After the 1993 World Trade Center bombing, Salem helped the FBI break up the cell, disrupting a jihadist plot to bomb New York City landmarks.

The second Egyptian officer—a stark contrast to Salem—was Ali Mohamed. He infiltrated the American military on behalf of Egyptian Islamic Jihad, stealing sensitive files that he took to New York, where he used them to help train the Blind Sheikh's cell. Later, Mohamed became al-Qaeda's top security specialist, helped bin Laden move his headquarters from Sudan to Afghanistan, forged the terror network's East African cells, and drew up the plans those cells later used to bomb the American embassy in Nairobi.[2]

In the Egyptian military, as in Egypt itself, sometimes you get Emad Salem . . . and sometimes you get Ali Mohamed.

---

2.   For biographical accounts of both Emad Salem and Ali Mohamed, see my book *Willful Blindness: A Memoir of the Jihad* (Encounter Books, paperback ed. 2009).

CHAPTER THIRTEEN

The Islamic Renaissance

Just after Mubarak fell, SCAF's transitional military government was put in place. The Muslim Brotherhood immediately announced the formation of the Freedom and Justice Party (*Hizb al-Hurriya wa al-'Adala*). That is, the Sunni supremacists used the same nomenclature—"justice," to connote sharia—that was applied in the naming of the AKP, Turkey's cognate "Justice and Development Party."

In so doing, they struck the same theme found in constitutions written for new "Islamic democracies"—such as Afghanistan's, where judges are primarily schooled in Islamic jurisprudence and swear an oath to sharia, to wit: "to support justice and righteousness in accord with the provisions of the sacred religion of Islam." Egypt's new party also invoked "freedom," consistent with the classic Brotherhood practice of sending different signals to different audiences. "Freedom" would play well with the Islamic Democracy Project crowd, which demands that Western taxpayers tune out the "Islamophobes" and pony up for the global spread of "liberty." Yet Muslims hearing the word would know that the Arab concept of "freedom"—"perfect slavery"—connoted submission, the essence of authoritarian Islam.[1]

SHHHH, DON'T TALK ABOUT THE FIRST FREE ELECTION

On March 21, the first day of spring 2011, there occurred what, to that point, was the most telling, most tellingly underreported, and most willfully misreported story of the "Arab Spring" saga: a national referendum on constitutional amendments. The vote, the first major, free election in the post-Mubarak Egypt and one in which eighteen million Egyptians participated, would determine the scheduling of elections for Parliament and a new president. It sounds dry, but it was crucial.

As we've noted, the Brotherhood is rigorously organized and disciplined, with an extensive network and deep roots in Egyptian life. Many of the Salafist factions, too, are longstanding and influential in pockets of the country. To the contrary, secular democratic reformers are in their infancy. Elections on a short schedule would obviously favor the Islamists; the real democrats need time—probably many years—to take root and grow.

The question of when to draft a new constitution put these two sides in direct conflict. The current 1971 Egyptian Constitution, suspended by the military immediately after Mubarak stepped down, was designed to keep the regime in power. Reformers wanted a new constitution written from scratch before any elections were held. Such an undertaking would have pushed elections a year or more into the future, in addition to giving the reformers more influence over the writing of the new constitution. The Brotherhood and the Salafists, by contrast, wanted elections held quickly. That would increase the chance that they'd win by large margins, rapidly take

---

1.   On "justice" in Islam and the new Afghan constitution, see Chapter 6 and Chapter 4.

power, and thus control a later constitution-writing process. The resulting law would be sure to have a distinctly Islamist flavor.

Consequently, under the Brotherhood's urging, a hastily assembled committee quickly cobbled together a few amendments (e.g., limiting presidents to two four-year terms) that would address some of the current constitution's major deficiencies. Islamists then argued that if Egyptians adopted these amendments, elections for parliament and then the presidency could proceed expeditiously, with the drafting of the new constitution to follow.

Significantly, they also contended that the proposed amendments would preserve the constitution's critical Article 2: "Islam is the Religion of the State, Arabic is its official language, and the principal source of legislation is Islamic jurisprudence." The last clause, enshrining sharia (and *fiqh*, the jurisprudence of sharia), was in the constitution because the Brotherhood had pressured Sadat to add it: the president first agreeing that sharia would be "*a* source" of legislation, then consenting to elevate it to "*the* principal source." These were crucial concessions, even if they were ones a dictator might find easy to make, dictators not being in the habit of allowing yesterday's concession to interfere with today's desire. As Professor Ran Hirschl argues, Sadat's constitutional changes "effectively transformed Egypt into a 'constitutional theocracy'"—borrowing a term Olivier Roy applied to Ayatollah Khomein's regime in Iran.[2] Article 2, naturally, is anathema to reformers. It is tremendously popular with the public at large, though, and therefore a very advantageous platform for an Islamist campaign.

The March 21 referendum enabled the country to vote the amendments up or down. Placed squarely before Egyptians, then, was a stark choice: the Islamic supremacist position or the secular

---

2.   Ran Hirschl, *Constitutional Courts v. Religious Fundamentalism* (University of Toronto Faculty of Law, Public Law and Legal Theory Research Paper No. 04-08), p. 6; see also, Ran Hirschl, *Constitutional Theocracy* (Harvard University Press 2010).

reform position. The referendum, in sum, was the perfect test of the Western party line that the "Arab Spring" is a spontaneous democratic uprising rather than the ascendancy of supremacist Islam.

Egypt being Egypt, the campaign was waged in the rhetoric of religious and cultural solidarity. On the "no" side were progressives, secular democrats, and non-Muslims. They were maligned in the mosques and Islamic centers as being "against Islam" and in cahoots with the Western hands said to be undermining the revolution. In fact, when Mohamed ElBaradei, one of the prominent figures on the "no" side, attempted to vote, he was pelted with rocks and had to find another polling station. By contrast, to favor the amendments and a rapid election schedule was to be "for Islam." Sheikh Qaradawi, for example, used his widely disseminated Friday sermon from Qatar to stump for a "yes" vote in Egypt.

In the event, the secular reformers were wiped out. The final tally in favor of the Islamists was a lopsided 78 to 22 percent. The referendum smashed the Arab Spring myth . . . so the myth's proponents ignored it. The vote was "merely procedural," most said—some jibber-jabber about scheduling arcana. Nothing to see here, move along. They were kidding themselves. The constitutional referendum perfectly foretold everything that has followed. The four-to-one ratio was revealing, too. It tracked to a T what polling tells us about the region: a strong majority of Muslims favors the imposition and enforcement of sharia. (See Chapter 5.)

After the Brotherhood's victory ensured that parliamentary elections would be held sooner rather than later, the outcome of those elections was a foregone conclusion. Within a few weeks, Amr Moussa, the Arab League leader and one of Egypt's most prominent politicians, flatly said that the Brotherhood's dominance was imminent: "It is inevitable that parliamentary elections . . . will usher in a legislature led by a bloc of Islamists, with the Brotherhood at the forefront."

JIHAD RETURNS TO THE SINAI FRONT

Even before the referendum, SCAF read the writing on the wall. The generals supported the Islamist position and continued consulting regularly with the Brotherhood about Egypt's future. In another ominous sign, in late May 2011, the transitional SCAF government marked the one-year anniversary of the *Mavi Marmara* "freedom flotilla" debacle (see Chapter 10) by announcing the reopening of the Rafah border crossing. This is the route into Gaza controlled by Egypt. Mubarak had ordered it closed in 2007, in conjunction with Israel's blockade, honoring Egypt's obligations under the Camp David Accord. His objective was to prevent the flow of weapons, personnel, and other support to Hamas. Now, with Islamists on the rise, the spigot was open again.

More alarming than the reopening of Rafah was the transitional government's abdication on the Sinai border with Israel, which, under Mubarak, had been heavily guarded to maintain the peace. In August, a team of up to twenty violent jihadists, some believed to be affiliated with al Qaeda, snaked into Sinai through secret tunnels from Gaza. Once there, they were either ignored or, worse, facilitated by Egyptian army forces as they hiked 200 kilometers toward the Israeli border at Eilat. The border there was porous; for thirty years, Israel had not needed to worry much about it.

After crossing into Israel, the jihadists took up positions along the highway and opened fire on buses and cars. One detonated a suicide belt. In all, eight Israelis were killed and thirty more wounded. The terrorists shot to death a family of four who were just out driving in their car: father, mother, and their six- and four-year-old kids—just a bit of "resistance" against the "occupiers," as Islamists like to say.

As is typical, Palestinians immediately began celebrating these atrocities, not only in Hamas-controlled Gaza but in the West Bank, where the "moderates" of Fatah are in charge. As the Israeli scholar

Barry Rubin noted at the time, "One Fatah site has such remarks as 'Our Lord is with the heroes'; 'I call for resistance in the Gaza with rocket fire and suicide bombings and the Glory of God and His Messenger'; 'Tribute to the Heroes of each attack and no matter what their affiliation'; 'God is great and victory is coming!'"

In a burgeoning "Islamic democracy," even a story such as this can always get worse. Israeli police and defense forces killed several of the terrorists. In hot pursuit of others, they crossed into Egyptian territory. A firefight ensued, at which point some Egyptian soldiers either joined it or got caught in it accidentally. When the smoke cleared, five Egyptian soldiers were dead.

Post-Mubarak Egypt erupted in rage. In early September, during an angry demonstration at the Israeli embassy in Cairo, a young man named Ahmed al-Shahat climbed twenty floors up the complex to reach the Israeli flag, which he tore down, replacing it with an Egyptian one. He was subsequently honored for heroism: hailed as "Flagman" and rewarded with a new home and job by the Governorate of Sharqiya in northern Egypt. A few days later, an angry mob stormed the Israeli embassy in Cairo, tearing down a protective wall, ransacking and burning the interior offices, beating embassy employees, and getting perilously close to the internal security area—to which Israelis who had not yet fled the premises had retreated. At long last, Egyptian security forces, which appear to have encouraged the riot, intervened to end it. An attack on a nation's embassy is, of course, an act of war—though Israeli Prime Minister Benjamin Netanyahu was quick to announce that Israel would continue adhering to the Camp David Accord.

SLEEPING WITH THE ENEMY

Like SCAF, the Obama administration also sought to work with the Brotherhood. The President's point-man on the scene, William Taylor, the State Department's "Special Coordinator for Middle East Transitions," acknowledged giving "training" to "Islamist parties" in the how-to's of popular elections. Later, he took pains to say the administration would be "satisfied" with a Muslim Brotherhood victory as long as elections were free and fair.

This anticipated satisfaction on the part of an American government was passing strange. In October 2010, just before the "Arab Spring" dominoes started falling in Tunis, the Brotherhood's Supreme Guide, Mohammed Badi, had given a speech calling for violent jihad against the United States. Specifically, Badi admonished Muslims to remember "Allah's commandment to wage jihad for His sake with [their] money and lives, so that Allah's word will reign supreme and the infidels' word will be inferior." Applying this injunction, Badi exclaimed that jihad, or "resistance," "is the only solution against the Zio-American arrogance and tyranny." On went the invective: The United States had been wounded by jihadists in Iraq and Afghanistan; thus, Badi gleefully surmised, America "is now experiencing the beginning of its end, and is heading towards its demise."

A few months later in Alexandria, Khairat el-Shater, Egypt's answer to Recep Tayyip Erdogan, began making himself heard. Shater is the Muslim Brotherhood's "Deputy General Guide." He is a charismatic figure, revered as the "Iron Man" for his defiant refusal to buckle through two decades of repeated detention and prosecution by Mubarak's regime, which branded him a money launderer and confiscated much of the fortune he'd amassed as a successful businessman. He also brings intellectual heft: after Mubarak fell, it was to Shater that the Brotherhood turned to craft its comprehensive strategy for shaping Egypt's future.

The Brothers have a name for this enterprise. It is called "the *Nahda* Project"—the Islamic "Renaissance."

In April 2011, Shater delivered a lengthy lecture, "Features of Nahda: Gains of the Revolution and the Horizons for Developing." Like Badi, Shater delivered his words in Arabic to like-minded Islamists—he was not speaking in English for Western consumption, as the Brothers do when they wish to appear as irenic pragmatists.

Shater's instruction was remarkable. He emphasized that the Brotherhood's fundamental principles and goals never change, only the tactics by which they are pursued. "You all know that our main and overall mission as Muslim Brothers is to empower God's religion on earth, to organize our life and the lives of the people on the basis of Islam, to establish the *Nahda* of the ummah and its civilization on the basis of Islam, and to subjugate people to God on earth." Shater went on to reaffirm the time-honored plan of the Brotherhood's founder, Hassan al-Banna, stressing the need for both personal piety and internal organizational discipline in pursuing the goal of worldwide Islamic hegemony.

The lecture dovetailed with a ninety-three-page platform released by the Brotherhood's Freedom and Justice Party, under the guidance of its leader Mohammed Morsi, a Shater confidant. The platform proposed to put every aspect of human life under sharia-compliant state regulation. The document was unmistakably anti-Western and anti-Israeli: structuring civil society on the foundation of "Arab and Islamic unity"; making the "strengthen[ing] of Arab and Islamic identity" the "goal of education"; making treaties (think: Camp David Accord) subject to approval by the population (i.e., the same population that had just, by a landslide, adopted the Islamist position on constitutional amendments); and describing Israel, "the Zionist entity, [as] an aggressive, expansionist, racist and settler entity."

CHOOSING ISLAMIC SUPREMACISM

Egypt's historic parliamentary elections took place in three stages, between the end of November 2011 and mid-January 2012. In late December 2011, with election returns already showing that Islamic supremacists would win a smashing victory, a jubilant Mohammed Badi (the aforementioned supreme guide of the Brotherhood) told the Egyptian press that the Brotherhood was close to achieving the "ultimate goal" set by Banna in 1928: the establishment of a "just and reasonable regime," which would be the stepping stone to "the establishment of a just Islamic caliphate." The new "ruling regime," he asserted, would strive to achieve one of Banna's key aims, "the establishment of a long-term plan for the reform of all aspects of people's lives." It would also exercise control over all the society's "institutions and elements." Badi had clearly brushed up on his Erdogan.

Islamic supremacists had their landslide victory. When the parliamentary election count was officially announced in January, it tracked almost exactly the Islamists' overwhelming win ten months earlier in the constitutional amendments referendum. Soon to be in firm control of the new government, the Brotherhood did what the wolf in sheep's clothing always does in triumph: It exploited its growing strength to take aggressive new positions, effectively demonstrating that its prior, ostensibly "moderate" stances were lies.

In the referendum over the amendments, the Brotherhood had reassured secular parties that postponing the writing of a new constitution until after the parliamentary and presidential elections would pose no threat to their interests. The drafting, the Brothers promised, would be an inclusive process: All strata of society—Islamist, modernist, non-Muslim, secular, progressive, etc.—would be represented in the "constituent assembly" that would draft the constitution. The Brothers feigned appreciation of the distinction between an ordinary piece of legislation and a constitution for the whole Egyptian people—the latter, they agreed, calls for a national consensus. Once the Brothers won control of the legislature, though, they and their Salafist coalition partners stacked the constituent assembly (the committee that would write the new constitution) with likeminded Islamic supremacists. Reformers protested, a number of them withdrawing from what had become a sham process.

After their smashing parliamentary victory, the Brothers also promptly went back on their commitment not to propose a candidate for the presidency. This reprised the sleight-of-hand they had successfully employed in connection with the legislative elections. Initially, to assuage fears of an Islamist takeover of the country, the Freedom and Justice Party promised to run for fewer than 50 percent of the seats in Parliament. The Brothers thus secured the transitional government's assent to their candidacy. Pocketing that benefit, they then upped the contested seat total to near 80 percent on the eve of the election, correctly surmising that if they contested more seats, the SCAF transitional government would put up no meaningful resistance, and thus the Brothers would end up dominating the legislature. Now, having pocketed control of Parliament and the constitution-writing process, they reversed themselves on the presidency, surmising that their candidate, the "Iron Man" himself, Khairat el-Shater, would stand a very good chance of winning. That would give them total control of the government.

As its grip tightened, the Brotherhood went back to one of its favorite topics, the Camp David Accords, flashing its trademark dissimulation. After the early rhetoric about canceling the peace treaty and preparing for war, the Brothers had put on their "pragmatic moderate" hats during the election campaign, repeating the mantra that the organization "respects international treaties." Now, however, with Parliament in the bag, the Brothers were shuffling again.

Rashad Bayoumi, Badi's deputy, told the *al-Hayat* newspaper in London that the Brotherhood's great respect for international treaties did not mean it would actually be *honoring* international treaties. It simply meant the issue of the peace treaty would be left "in the hands of the people." They, after all, had not been consulted when Sadat signed Camp David. "All parties can reconsider the treaty and Egyptians haven't yet had their say," Boyoumi rationalized. Though he maintained that the Brotherhood would not "violate the treaty," it seemed that violations were in the eye of the beholder. It would not be a "violation" evidently, for the treaty to be abrogated by a "referendum among the people or Parliament." Of course, he and the Brothers knew full well that both the Egyptian people and the

Parliament—which the people had just stacked with a four-to-one Islamist majority—would vote overwhelmingly against the pact. Asked about recognizing Israel's right to exist, Bayoumi shot back, "I'll never allow myself to sit down with a criminal. We will not deal with Israelis by any means."

"UNALTERABLY OPPOSED?" NAH, WE CAN WORK WITH THESE GUYS

Moderate? The United States government apparently thought so. The Obama administration was chomping at the bit to sit down with the Brotherhood. Laying the "no problem here" groundwork, Bruce Reidl, a key Obama adviser on Middle East policy, came flying out of the box with a *Daily Beast* essay, "Don't Fear Egypt's Muslim Brotherhood" (to which I duly responded with a *National Review* essay, "Fear the Muslim Brotherhood"). Meanwhile, a "senior" Obama administration official told the *New York Times* that it would be "totally impractical" not to engage with the Brotherhood since the Brothers were "the party that won the election," and "they've been very specific about conveying a moderate message." Shades of Neville Chamberlain.

The *Times*, a reliable administration mouthpiece, made no mention of the Brotherhood's Palestinian terrorist division, Hamas, or of its recent reaffirmation of the goal of a global caliphate, or of its threat to torpedo the Camp David Accord by referendum, etc., etc. The paper instead twaddled about the Brotherhood's "repeated assurances" that it would "respect individual freedoms, free markets and international commitments, including Egypt's treaty with Israel." Fresh from meeting with top leaders of the Brotherhood's Freedom and Justice Party, Senator John Kerry, the Foreign Relations Committee chairman, former Democratic presidential nominee, and Obama adviser, chirped, "You're certainly going to have to figure out how to deal with democratic governments that don't espouse every policy or value you have."

Not to be outdone, progressive Republicans also sang the Brotherhood's praises. A year earlier, Senator John McCain of Arizona had insisted, during an interview by the German newspaper *Der Spiegel*, that the Muslim Brotherhood was "a radical group that, first of all, supports Sharia law; that in itself is anti-democratic—at least as far as women are concerned. They have been involved with other terrorist organizations and I believe that they should be specifically excluded from any transition government." Around the same time, McCain's oft-time side-kick, Senator Lindsey Graham of South Carolina, chimed in that he was suspicious of the Brothers' "agenda" and that "their motives are very much in question." Ah, but that was then.

While the parliamentary election was still underway, but after it was clear that the Brotherhood would win big, the SCAF transition government provoked a crisis by charging a number of "civil society activists," including sixteen Americans, with violating a Mubarak-era law that forbade NGOs in Egypt from accepting foreign funding. Among the Americans prohibited from leaving Egypt pending trial was Sam Lahood, the son of Transportation Secretary Ray Lahood, the only Republican in President Obama's cabinet. The American NGOs in violation of the law included the International Republican Institute, a progressive endowment that is a clearinghouse for channeling millions of American taxpayer dollars for democracy promotion and "civil society development" across the globe. The IRI had also been a McCain fiefdom since he was named its chairman in the early Nineties. McCain thus trouped over to Egypt with Graham and other lawmakers in tow, seeking to resolve the dispute.

Mirabile dictu, they found fast friends in . . . the Muslim Brotherhood. Suddenly, the GOP senators were glowing over their new allies. As the *Wall Street Journal* reported, McCain and his delegation "hinted at warming relations between conservative [ahem] American lawmakers and the Muslim Brotherhood." "After talking with the Muslim Brotherhood," Senator Graham cooed, "I was struck with their commitment to change the [NGO] law because they believe it's unfair." No kidding. The Islamist organization's opposition to the regime and fondness for foreign funding had been among the primary reasons Mubarak had put the law in place . . . though it had not, until now, been enforced it against organizations tied to the U.S. government. Graham elaborated: "I was very apprehensive when I heard the election results" that gave the Brotherhood a commanding grip on power. "But after visiting and talking with the Muslim Brotherhood I am hopeful that . . . we can have a relationship with Egypt where the Muslim Brotherhood is a strong political voice."

Yes indeed, Happy Spring!

The SCAF transition government provoked the NGO crisis for an obvious reason: To squeeze the United States. At issue was whether our government would continue to lavish close to $1.5 billion per year in American taxpayer funds on the Egyptian military. The funding had been put in doubt by both the Muslim Brotherhood's electoral success and SCAF's failure to make sufficient progress towards democracy, a condition Congress had placed on the funding in order to promote freedom of speech, religion and association, as well as due process of law.

The civil society activists were finally released after tense negotiations: the Obama administration essentially paid a $5 million bribe—the required "bail" for lifting the travel ban. The Arabic press also claimed, however, that one of the topics that arose during the negotiations was the notion of a swap: the activists would be released if the Americans released a number of Egyptian prisoners in U.S. jails, including Sheikh Omar Abdel Rahman, "the Blind Sheikh" serving a life sentence in connection with the 1993 World Trade Center bombing, a plot to kill Mubarak, and various other jihadist conspiracies. The activists were released after the "bail" was paid. Further, in April 2012, the Obama administration quietly announced that the annual American pot of gold for Egypt's military would be paid. There was no mention of a prisoner swap . . . but, as we shall see, that hardly meant the topic was a dead letter.

THE BROTHERHOOD'S PLAN B

For its part, SCAF was becoming increasingly alarmed at the prospect of total Muslim Brotherhood power over the state. It had been working with the Brothers and, like the Spring Fever West, seeing them as inevitable but maybe controllable: "pragmatic" extremists with whom it might be possible to cut a deal that preserved the military's most important privileges, funding, and business interests. The generals knew from both long experience and recent history, however, that the Brothers were not trustworthy, that their long-term goal—and perhaps even their *short-term* goal—was complete control of the government, very much including dominance over the military. The Islamists' success was just making them more power-hungry. Egypt's generals knew well the Turkish template. It was time to put some up some roadblocks and stop the momentum.

With a new tranche of American funding now secured, SCAF moved to block Shater and other Islamist candidates from the presidency. A SCAF-appointed cat's paw, the Supreme Presidential Election Commission (SPEC) ruled that Shater was disqualified from seeking office on the laughable grounds that he had laundered money for a "banned group" to which he illegally belonged. It's not that he was innocent—he wasn't. But he'd been given a pardon on the money laundering after Mubarak was ousted, and the "banned group" in question, the Muslim Brotherhood, was now not only un-banned, *it had been elected to run Parliament.*

In addition, SPEC tossed from the presidential race a popular Islamist, Hazem Abu-Ismail, whom the military dreaded because he appealed to both Salafist and Brotherhood supporters. Abu-Ismail's alleged deficiency was that his mother had been a dual citizen of the United States. This was said to flout the requirement that a candidate's parents not be foreign nationals, even though Shater's mother was plainly an Egyptian citizen. To make it look even-handed, SPEC also excluded Omar Suleiman, the Mubarak regime's former intelligence chief, citing fraudulent nominating signature-petitions. I believe I had a better chance of winning than he did. (As it happened, Suleiman was also in failing health—he died shortly after the presidential election.)

Despite Brotherhood huffing and puffing, the transitional government's decision was final: Shater was out. As is always the case, however, the Brothers had a Plan B. With little fanfare, they had proposed a second candidate, an alternative just in case there had been problems with Shater. He was Mohamed Morsi, the aforementioned head of the Freedom and Justice Party. A sixty-year-old engineer and academic who lacks Shater's magnetism, Morsi is nonetheless a force to be reckoned with. He is also a testament to the American infrastructure that the Brotherhood has steadily built for the last half century.

As his wife, Nagla Ali Mahmoud, would later relate to the Associated Press, the American-educated Morsi pursued his doctorate at the University of Southern California in the early Eighties. His wife soon joined him in the Golden State. In fact, two of the five Morsi children are American citizens, having been born in the U.S. More significantly for present purposes, it was in California that Morsi and his wife joined the Muslim Brotherhood, apparently through the Muslim Students Association. The MSA is the first building block of the Brotherhood's American foundation and the gateway through which many young Muslims begin what Hudson's Samuel Tadros describes as the lengthy process of study and service that leads to membership—a process "designed to ensure with absolute certainty that there is conformity to the movement's ideology and a clear adherence to its leadership's authority."

For the historic Egyptian presidential election, Morsi was a condign choice as the Brotherhood's fallback plan. He is a Shater protégé whose rise in the organization, and to the leadership of the Brotherhood's Freedom and Justice Party, owed to the backing of his revered patron, as well as to Morsi's own firm belief in the organization's traditions of discipline and obedience to hierarchical superiors. He was twice jailed, for brief intervals, during Mubarak's reign. He is also said to have had a difficult relationship with a rebellious group of young Brothers expelled from the organization during the Tahrir Square uprisings. Morsi adheres fiercely to classical sharia—reportedly, part of his dispute with the renegades involved his support for hardline Brotherhood positions that women and non-Muslims should be barred from running for president and that laws should be vetted by religious scholars. As a parliamentarian during Mubarak's reign, moreover, he bitterly opposed the regime's energy trade with Israel (Egypt provides 40 percent of Israel's natural gas), in addition to arguing that pro-American elements in the regime were trying to weaken both Islamic education and the influence of al-Azhar scholars.

Notably, Morsi's wife is a longtime, influential member of the Muslim Sisterhood, the distaff division of the Brotherhood. She customarily wears what is, essentially, the Sisterhood's hyper-modest uniform: a drab headscarf (or hijab) and black robe (or abaya). Eventually, she rose to a high-level post in the Sisterhood's "Guidance Bureau." Interestingly, another member of the Guidance Bureau is Saleha Abedin—who just happens to be the mother of Huma Abedin, Secretary of State Clinton's deputy chief of staff and close adviser.[3] Small world, no? It was Mrs. Clinton, recall, who pronounced it "imperative" that the Egyptian military turn over power to the country's newly elected leaders.

During the Egyptian presidential campaign, before SCAF excluded Shater from contention, Morsi was a constant presence at Shater's side. Significantly, he was introduced to crowds as an "architect" of Shater's "Nahda" program—the Brotherhood's Islamic Renaissance plan for Egypt's future. As Morsi rose through the ranks in his Brotherhood career, Shater was in the background, pushing

---

3. Huma Abedin is married to another Clinton family confidant, Anthony Weiner, the New York Democrat forced to resign from Congress due to a scandal.

Morsi forward. Now, with Shater forced to the background, Morsi moved forward once more.

Dr. Morsi was the most important candidate connected to the Brotherhood's American operation, but he was not the only one. Bassem Khafagi also tossed his keffiyeh in the ring. Prior to launching a career in Egyptian politics, Khafagi was CAIR's "community affairs director." He was also a founder of the Islamic Assembly of North America, a Michigan-based organization notorious for endorsing al Qaeda figures, promoting sharia, and defending female genital mutilation. Regrettably, Khafagi's American career as an Islamist community organizer was cut short when what surely must have been a misunderstanding led him to plead guilty in Detroit federal court to bank and visa fraud charges. But then the silver lining: he was deported to Egypt where, presto, "Islamic democracy" had him running for president. Though he did not win, Khafagi did have an exciting platform, calling for "the complete implementation of Islamic law"—you know, the thing CAIR says only an "Islamophobe" would claim CAIR and the rest of the Brotherhood's American network aspire to.

"THE SHARIA, THEN THE SHARIA, AND FINALLY, THE SHARIA!"

With all the attention riveted to Shater and then to his controversial disqualification from the presidential race, Morsi was given little chance. The election, after all, was scheduled for late May—just a few weeks away. It seemed awfully late in the game for a heretofore unnoticed candidate to gain traction. In fact, when a high profile debate was televised in mid-May, Morsi was not even among the participants. Instead, two better known contenders, the Brotherhood's former operative Abdel Abol-Fotouh and the regime's former foreign minister Amr Moussa, jousted. They show that there is some consensus in all Egyptian political debate these days: the two mutually agreed that the peace treaty with Israel should be reviewed.

In the interim, back at Tahrir Square, Islamic supremacist agitators staged a demonstration to protest SCAF's interference in the election. Participating along with the Brotherhood was the Islamic Group (*al-Gama'at al-Islamiya*), the terrorist organization led by the imprisoned Blind Sheikh. In Egypt's new "Islamic democracy," the Islamic Group is now considered just another Salafist "political" movement. Among the protest leaders lambasting the military for hijacking the revolution was Muhammad al-Zawahiri—the brother of the infamous al Qaeda chief Ayman al-Zawahiri. Muhammad had only recently been released after serving fourteen years on terrorism charges. The protesters waved banners that read, "We are a people who do not give in—Victory or Death!" and chanted "Jihad! Jihad! The [Military] Council must leave!"—"all punctuated," the superb analyst Ray Ibrahim notes, "by cries of Islam's primordial war-cry, '*Allahu Akbar!*'"

The rising anger against the military among the nation's fundamentalists worked greatly to Morsi's benefit. So did the Brotherhood's incomparable network throughout Egypt. If SCAF thought it had successfully dodged a bullet by sidelining Shater, it badly underestimated both Morsi and his organization. A few days before the presidential election, he thrilled a like-minded throng and television audience by hammering home the Brotherhood's long-time ambitions. MEMRI provided a translation, with these highlights:

> **Morsi:** [In the 1920's, when Hassan al-Banna founded the Muslim Brotherhood, the Egyptians] said: "The constitution is our Koran." They wanted to show that the constitution is a great thing. But Imam al-Banna, Allah's mercy upon him, said to them: "No, the Koran is our constitution."
>
> The Koran was and will continue to be our constitution. The Koran will continue to be our constitution. The Koran *is* our constitution.
>
> **Crowd:** The Koran is our constitution.
> **Morsi:** The Prophet Mohammed is our leader.
> **Crowd:** The Prophet Mohammed is our leader.

Morsi: Jihad is our path.

Crowd: Jihad is our path.

Morsi: And death for the sake of Allah is our most lofty aspiration.

Crowd: And death for the sake of Allah is our most lofty aspiration.

Morsi: Above all—Allah is our goal.

Morsi later continued with a vow that, under his guidance, the new Egyptian constitution would reflect true sharia:

> The sharia, then the sharia, and finally, the sharia. This nation will enjoy blessing and revival only through the Islamic sharia. I take an oath before Allah and before you all that regardless of the actual text [of the constitution] . . . Allah willing, the text will truly reflect [the sharia], as will be agreed upon by the Egyptian people, by the Islamic scholars, and by legal and constitutional experts. . . . Rejoice and rest assured that this people will not accept a text that does not reflect the true meaning of the Islamic sharia as a text to be implemented and as a platform. The people will not agree to anything else.

Recall that the classical sharia manual, *Reliance of the Traveller*, was endorsed by Islamic scholars at al-Azhar University, as well as the Muslim Brotherhood's think-tank, the International Institute of Islamic Thought. Recall, too, that the Brotherhood's most influential sharia jurist is none other than Sheikh Yusuf Qaradawi. *That* is Morsi's sharia.

Morsi's gut-level appeal to the Brotherhood's first principles served him extraordinarily well. When the votes were tallied in the presidential election's first phase (May 23-24, 2012), he was declared the winner, garnering 26 percent. This meant he would face the runner-up in a final showdown in June.

Severalcommentators tried to spin the Brotherhood's victory as somehow a negative for the organization, reasoning that it was a significant plummet from the 50 percent the Brothers had scored in the parliamentary election. Such analyses—from which we were to infer that secular democratic forces might finally be stirring— were specious. Remember, Morsi was an afterthought: a Brotherhood contingency plan who got next to no attention until the last minute when a better known, more appealing candidate was ousted. Yet, he won anyway. Furthermore, by winning, the Brotherhood humiliated SCAF, which had tried to scotch its chances. Morsi's 26 percent showing was impressive, moreover, given that the field was crowded by *thirteen candidates*; indeed, the wide array of choices is why 26 percent was enough to win by three points, not a small margin under the circumstances. Nor did Morsi's tally indicate that Islamists were losing their grip; the remaining Islamist vote simply split among Salafist candidates—or stayed home because SCAF tried to rig the election by excluding Shater and Abu-Ismail, the preferred supremacist candidates.

One Arab Spring enthusiast, the admirable journalist and scholar Amir Taheri, stressed the surprisingly low voter turnout, 42 percent, in rationalizing that Morsi's showing computed to only 11 percent support from the total population. Such a facile analysis fell way below Taheri's usual standards, risibly inferring that every person who fails to vote is a "no" vote. Let's pretend, however, Taheri was right. What does his "low turnout" algorithm say about the strength of *realdemocracy* in Egypt?

For anyone seized by Spring Fever, anyone fallen under the spell of "Islamic democracy" as a Sherman's march of liberty through tyranny, the presidential election's first phase should have been the cure. A McClatchy News dispatch from Cairo—more of a *cri de coeur*— captured the moment well. The "revolutionaries"—the report's label for the tech-savvy, secular, progressive, Facebook twenty-somethings the press still insists drove the uprising, no matter how many referenda betray them as a negligible factor—were "stunned and shattered as the first democratic election [in Egypt] rejected their calls, instead producing a runoff between one candidate who wants an Islamic-based state and another who promises a return to the deposed regime."[4]

Yes, the second-place finisher, Ahmed Shafiq, was no secular democrat. He is Mubarak's former prime minister. The "revolutionaries," the McClatchy report grudgingly conceded, "didn't truly understand popular Egyptian sentiment." In this "Islamic democracy," that sentiment substantially breaks down to non-democratic Islamists versus the non-democratic regime.

Was there an ebb in Brotherhood support? Many Egyptians, including many Islamists, were surely turned off by the Brotherhood's duplicity in running a presidential candidate after saying it would not do so. That, no doubt, trimmed some of Morsi's support, albeit not nearly enough to stop him from winning. But the Brotherhood has to be distinguished here from the broader Islamist movement that it leads but does not completely control (which is why the Salafists won 25 percent of the vote in the parliamentary election). Support for Islamic supremacism remained palpable; a goodly chunk of it just split among Islamist candidates other than the Brotherhood candidate.

FREE THE BLIND SHEIKH

The eye-opener in the election was the 23 percent showing by the regime operative who was SCAF's clear choice. Ahmed Shafiq is a Mubarak chum: a former air force commander who, as the Associated Press noted, "campaigned overtly as the 'anti-revolution' candidate." His obvious appeal to voters "would have been inconceivable

---

4.   In the media's telling, not only is Egypt's Arab Spring still driven by Facebook "revolutionaries"; the regime has been "deposed." It is worth noting that what has been deposed is Mubarak. The regime, which is to say, the military, is still very much intact . . . *at least for now*, as Recep Tayyip Erdogan might say.

a year ago amid the public's anti-regime fervor." But after fifteen months of watching the Islamic "Nahda" that Egypt's Islamist masses were choosing when given the chance, the frightened remainder of the population was not choosing real democracy as an alternative vision. In this undemocratic region, real democracy does not stand a chance against Islamic supremacism. If we apply Amir Taheri's analytical formula, support for it is in the single digits. What non-Islamist Egyptians crave is security and stability. They were beginning to turn to the only people in the country who might be able to give it to them: the military hardliners.

Naturally, Obama administration officials did not see it that way. In mid-June, they played host in Washington to a delegation of Egypt's new leaders, including top Brotherhood officials and other leading Islamists. To pull off this dialogue about the future of the country and the region, the administration issued travel visas for the delegation, including one for Hani Nour Eldin. There was just one problem: Eldin, a "Salafist" newly elected to Parliament, is actually a member of the Islamic Group, the aforementioned terrorist organization led by the imprisoned Omar Abdel Rahman, the "Blind Sheikh."

Some history is in order. In 1997, a year after Abdel Rahman was sentenced to life imprisonment for pioneering the terror cell that bombed the Wolrd Trade Center, the Islamic Group threatened to "target . . . all of those Americans who participated in subjecting [Abdel Rahman's] life to danger"—"every American official, starting with the American president [down] to the despicable jailer." The organization promised to do "everything in its power" to obtain its emir's release. Six months later, Islamic Group jihadists set upon fifty-eight foreign tourists and several police officers at an archeological site in Luxor, Egypt, brutally shooting and slicing them to death. The terrorists left behind leaflets—including in the mutilated torso of one victim—demanding that the Blind Sheikh be freed.

Subsequently, the Islamic Group issued a statement warning that its forcible struggle against the Egyptian regime would proceed unless Mubarak met its three demands: the implementation of sharia, the cessation of diplomatic relations with Israel, and "the return of our Sheikh and emir to his land." In March 2000, terrorists associated with the Abu Sayyaf group kidnapped a number of tourists in the Philippines and threatened to behead them if Abdel Rahman and two other convicted terrorists were not freed. Authorities later recovered two decapitated bodies (four other hostages were never accounted for).

On September 21, 2000, only three weeks before al Qaeda's bombing of the U.S.S. *Cole*, al-Jazeera televised a "Convention to Support the Honorable Omar Abdel Rahman." Front and center were Osama bin Laden and Ayman al-Zawahiri (then bin Laden's deputy, now the late al Qaeda emir's successor). They warned that unless Sheikh Abdel Rahman was freed, jihadist attacks against the United States would be stepped up. At the same event, Mohammed Abdel Rahman, an al-Qaeda operative who is one of the Blind Sheikh's sons, exhorted the crowd to "avenge your Sheikh" and "go to the spilling of blood."

In the immediate aftermath of the 9/11 attacks, the *New York Post* reported bin Laden's proclamation that his war on America had been justified by a fatwa promulgated by Abdel Rahman from prison. The Blind Sheikh had indeed issued a decree casting the fight for his release as an Islamic duty. Regarding Americans, he directed:

> Muslims everywhere to dismember their nation, tear them apart, ruin their economy, provoke their corporations, destroy their embassies, attack their interests, sink their ships, . . . shoot down their planes, [and] kill them on land, at sea, and in the air. Kill them wherever you find them.

In Egypt's new "Islamic democracy," the Islamic Group (and its new arm, the "Building and Development Party") may be seen as a "political party." In the United States, however, its atrocious record makes the Islamic Group a formally designated foreign terrorist organization. Providing it material support—such as overlooking its prohibited status and issuing it travel authorization to pursue its agenda in the United States—is a felony, the crime of material support to terrorism. Not long ago, the United States government prosecuted the Blind Sheikh's lawyer, Lynne Stewart, for providing material support to terrorism by helping the Islamic Group receive guidance from its imprisoned leader. Though in her seventies, Stewart was given a ten-year jail sentence. Nevertheless, in our current Spring Fever epidemic, Obama officials have cut out the middleman: Now, the Islamic Group gets its material support directly from the federal government.

The White House and State Department stonewalled media inquiries about how a man well known to be a member of a formally designated terrorist organization could conceivably have been issued, first, a visa to enter the United States, and then, an invitation to consult with our government's security and foreign policy officials in Washington. A State Department spokeswoman stammered that, however it may have happened, it was really no big deal because, after all, Hani Nour Eldin had been democratically elected. All we do know is that Eldin used his audience with senior Obama aides, including the deputy national security adviser, to press for the release and repatriation of the Blind Sheikh. To return him to Egypt, Eldin said, "would be a gift to the revolution."

GIVE ME SECURITY OR GIVE ME . . . THE "ARAB SPRING"

Meanwhile back in Egypt, Mohammed Badi, was at it again. While the White House consulted with the "largely secular" Brotherhood "moderates," their Supreme Guide was calling for the destruction of Israel. "Every Muslim," he declared, "will be asked about the Zionists' usurpation of al-Aqsa Mosque. Why did he not seek to recover it, and wage jihad in [Allah's] way? Did he not care about the fatwa of the ulema [scholars] of the Muslims: 'Jihad of self and

174

money to recover al Aqsa is a duty on every Muslim'?" He exhorted "all Muslim rulers" to make "the Palestinian cause a pivotal issue," and predicted new "freedom flotillas" would break the "murdering Zionist criminals."

Though the first phase of the presidential election showed that many alarmed Egyptians preferred the regime to the Islamists, SCAF was resigned to its preferred candidate's defeat. The junta knew the Egyptian landscape. It knew there simply was not enough non-Islamist support. The run-off would not be like the first-round, a race with numerous candidates, under circumstances where the transitional government could pick off the most popular Islamists. This would be one-on-one, the regime (Shafiq) against the Brotherhood (Morsi). The generals knew that unless they stole the election, they were virtually certain to lose it. With all the Arab Spring delirium equating elections with the Holy Grail of "democracy," with all the damage and instability caused by months of Tahrir Square demonstrations, the generals were not willing to steal the election outright. Nor did they have the nerve to cancel it. Instead, they did what they saw as the next best thing: The decisive presidential election would go forward, but its significance would be markedly undercut.

SCAF thus issued the edict that, Turkey's Prime Minister Erdogan declaimed, "parliamentarian democracy will never accept." On June 14, it dissolved parliament. The historic popular election had occurred, but its effect was nullified, as was the Islamists' hammerlock on the writing of a new constitution—which, the generals decreed, would now be handled by a committee of SCAF's choosing. The final round of the presidential election would go forward, but without a parliament there would be no law for a president to enforce, and without a constitution the president's powers would not be defined. The only thing that would remain certain was the power of the military, which would remain in charge even if a few elections had to be held to give the regime the ornaments of "democracy." It was as if Mubarak had never left.

The Brotherhood was outraged. Erdogan was outraged. The Obama administration and European leaders were outraged. The "revolutionaries" again came to Tahrir Square—outraged, of course, but now more jaded than energized. There was and would be continuing pressure on the junta to relent. Senior Obama officials would finger-wag about how imperative it was that the military surrender power to Egypt's democratically elected leaders . . . but only after continuing to fund the military in a manner that enabled it to thumb its nose at Egypt's democratically elected leaders. The generals are teetering. They will fade a lot faster than Ataturk's generals did. Their time, though, is not over. Not yet.

Much of its thunder stolen, the run-off election went forward three days after the dissolution order. As widely predicted, Morsi prevailed. After SCAF's diminishment of the exercise, turnout was low, clearly depressing Islamist support and buoying the regime's. Still, Morsi won by nearly a million votes, 52 to 48 percent—interestingly, getting a strong boost from the expatriate vote, including from Egyptians living in the United States, which broke four-to-one for the Islamic supremacist candidate.

As non-Islamists shuddered, Egypt's secular parties condemned the United States government for what they aptly perceived as its endorsement of the Muslim Brotherhood. Nevertheless, President Obama was quick to join Turkey's prime minister, as well as Erdogan's fellow Islamic supremacist leaders, such as Hezbollah, in congratulating President-elect Morsi. Senator John Kerry also assured Americans that, "in our discussions, Mr. Morsi committed to protecting fundamental freedoms, including women's rights, minority rights, the right to free expression and assembly, and he said he understood the importance of Egypt's post-revolutionary relationships with America and Israel."

Morsi apparently didn't get the memo. In his first public speech as president-elect, addressing tens of thousands of Islamist supporters, he pledged to pressure the United States to free the Blind

Shiekh and return him home to Egypt. Now there's a man with his priorities in order.

Days later, as Morsi and the Obama administration publicly pressured the transitional military junta to transfer power to the newly elected president, it was announced that the Muslim Brotherhood and the Salafist parties had agreed: Egypt would be ruled by sharia. Not by "the principles of sharia," a slippery phrase that Islamic supremacists revile as an end-run around Allah's law. No, any new constitution would make clear that sharia *is* the law. Period.

In Egypt, the train is nearing its destination.

It's How You Think About It

Writing a book about the "Arab Spring" in the mid-summer of 2012 is akin to drawing conclusions about a lop-sided World Series after three games have been played: Barring a miracle, we already know the outcome even though we also know there are many more innings yet to be played.

The ascendancy of Islamic supremacism underway in the Middle East will take many years to play out. Turkey tells us how it will end. Egypt shows us that the "Turkish Model"—*Islamization*, not *democratization*—will work much more rapidly in an Arab Muslim society. Yet even Turkey remains a work in regress: Prime Minister Erdogan has moved his country back into the Islamist camp, but the imposition of sharia inside Turkey is far from complete. In Egypt, the Islamists have only gotten started degrading the resistance of the military, an imperative Erdogan has largely achieved, but only after several years.

The objective of this book is not to relate a definitive history of the "Arab Spring." That would impossible at this early stage. The objective is to offer an alternative way of thinking about the phenomenon that is unfolding before our eyes. It is to realize that the "Arab Spring" is not unprecedented, and that the precedents we have, especially Turkey, illustrate that the advance of Islam is the very opposite of a forward march of freedom. It is, moreover, to understand why this must be the case: to confront the seminal role of classical sharia in shaping Islamist movements—to understand that what makes these movements *supremacist* is a depressingly mainstream construction of Islamic sharia and scripture.

Finally, we must come to grips with how deeply the progressive devolution of democracy has warped our understanding of what democracy is. Conventional wisdom has sapped the spirit of liberty that was Western democracy's defining feature. Totalitarian democracy is not real democracy. But if we have become bereft of the capacity to tell them apart, we will surely continue to look with hope at that which we should dread. That is Spring Fever: hallucinating the Muslim Brotherhood's "civilization jihad," with its deep anti-American and rabid anti-Semitic roots, into an "Arab Spring."

Beyond Turkey, beyond Egypt, Islamists are on the rise. It was in Tunisia that the latest Arab Spring began. Long recognized as the most Westernized of Arab nations, it is now firmly in the control of a Muslim Brotherhood offshoot spearheaded by Rachid Ghannouchi. The group is called the "Nahda" movement (*Hizb ut Nahda*, also known as the "Ennahda Party")—yes, just like Khairat el-Shater's fundamentalist blueprint for an Islamic "Renaissance" that the Egyptian Muslim Brotherhood is trying to implement. No surprise there: as we saw, Ghannouchi was a featured eminence at Brotherhood conferences in Istanbul.

Ghannouchi has a long history of supporting the annihilation of what he calls "the germ of Israel," and of supporting Hamas terrorism toward that end. "To strike at Zionism in Palestine," he has written, "is to strike at the enemy in its new citadel." Along with the heads of Hamas, Hezbollah, and the Muslim Brotherhood, he has signed a statement declaring: "The bodies of the men and women of Palestine are shields against the Zionist agenda, which its greater target is to destroy the entire Islamic Ummah." Yet he is now lionized by the *New York Times* as "a progressive Muslim leader," and feted by officials of the same American government he once, from Iran, called "the greatest danger to civilization." As this is written, he has just stressed, lest anyone got the wrong idea, that Tunisia will never recognize Israel's right to exist. Ghannouchi points to Turkey as his "model" for Tunisia's "Islamic democracy." He's clearly got something there: the new Nahda government has just begun prosecuting Tunisians for "insulting the sacred"—two men were just sentenced to over seven years' imprisonment for posting unflattering cartoons of Mohammed.

In Libya, the United States intervened to enable Islamic supremacists led by the Brotherhood and al Qaeda to topple and brutally murder Moammar Qaddafi. To be sure, Qaddafi was a loathsome dictator with American blood on his hands. But in 2003, after he abandoned his nuclear program, it was the United States that brought him in from the cold, embraced him as a "valuable ally" against terrorism due to the intelligence he provided about Libya's teeming jihadist strongholds, and provided foreign aid to support his military dictatorship. Yet, the very same American politicians who, in August 2009, were in Qaddafi's Tripoli compound celebrating the alliance between Libya and the United States—Republican Senators John McCain and Lindsey Graham, to cite two—were only eighteen months later calling for him to be bombed into submission so Libyans could finally experience "Islamic democracy." The country has now descended into violent chaos. Qaddafi's former arsenal has been raided and parsed out to al Qaeda and Hamas, among other violent jihadists.

Spring Fever, unfortunately, is an incurable condition for some. As this is written, our transnational progressive visionaries, fresh from their Libyan "success," now urge a repeat performance in

Syria—where the Muslim Brotherhood opposition, with the open support of al Qaeda, Hamas, Turkey, and Saudi Arabia, is in a fierce struggle to overthrow the barbaric Assad regime.

The Obama administration is torn between its "Islamic democracy" yearnings and its election year need to avoid another mess akin to Libya. So, while it lends the Syrian Islamists covert support, it remains on the sidelines. In this paralysis, however unintentionally, we've achieved the soundest foreign policy in memory: our fractious enemies are fighting against, and weakening, each other rather than uniting against America as they usually do. But the bipartisan progressive clerisy continues to demand American intervention and "democracy" promotion—even if the "democracy" that results is rabidly anti-American. Spring turns out to be an endless season.

The Muslim Middle East is aflame, not with democracy but with Islamic supremacist ideology. When the conflagration will end and exactly what each theater will look like once it does, we cannot say for sure. We know only that classical sharia is being seared into the region's fabric. Necessarily, that means it will be more hostile to the West, more anti-American, and more committed to Israel's destruction. Necessarily, "Islamic democracy" will make the Middle East less democratic, and less free.

ABOUT THE AUTHOR

Andrew C. McCarthy was a top federal prosecutor involved in some of the most significant cases in recent history. Decorated with the Justice Department's highest honors, he retired from government in 2003, after helping to launch the investigation into the 9/11 terrorist attacks. He is one of America's most persuasive voices on national security issues and author of the bestsellers *Willful Blindness: A Memoir of the Jihad* and *The Grand Jihad: How Islam and the Left Sabotage America*. He is the executive director of the Philadelphia Freedom Center and a senior fellow at the National Review Institute. He writes the Ordered Liberty column for PJ Media, and is a contributing editor at *National Review* and *The New Criterion*. You can keep up to date with his work at www.andrewcmccarthy. com.